Brown, Warren

The search for the Northwest
passage

The Search for the
Northwest Passage

General Editor

William H. Goetzmann
Jack S. Blanton, Sr., Chair in History
    University of Texas at Austin

Consulting Editor

Tom D. Crouch
Chairman, Department of Aeronautics
    National Air and Space Museum
    Smithsonian Institution

WORLD EXPLORERS

The Search for the
Northwest Passage

Warren Brown

Introductory Essay by Michael Collins

CHELSEA HOUSE PUBLISHERS

New York · Philadelphia

On the cover Sixteenth-century French map of Canada and portrait of Martin Frobisher.

Chelsea House Publishers
Editor-in-Chief Remmel Nunn
Managing Editor Karyn Gullen Browne
Copy Chief Juliann Barbato
Picture Editor Adrian G. Allen
Art Director Maria Epes
Deputy Copy Chief Mark Rifkin
Assistant Art Director Noreen Romano
Manufacturing Manager Gerald Levine
Systems Manager Lindsey Ottman
Production Manager Joseph Romano
Production Coordinator Marie Claire Cebrián

World Explorers
Senior Editor Sean Dolan

Staff for THE SEARCH FOR THE NORTHWEST PASSAGE
Copy Editor Philip Koslow
Editorial Assistant Martin Mooney
Picture Researcher Joan Beard
Senior Designer Basia Niemczyc

First Printing

1 3 5 7 9 8 6 4 2

Library of Congress Cataloging-in-Publication Data

Brown, Warren.
The search for the Northwest passage / Warren Brown.
p.   cm.—(World explorers)
Includes bibliographical references and index.
Summary: An account of the search for and discovery of the
Northwest Passage.
ISBN 0-7910-1297-2
    0-7910-1530-0 (pbk.)
1. Northwest Passage—Juvenile literature. [1. Northwest Passage.]
I. Title. II. Series.   90-2245
G640.B76 1990   CIP
910′.9163′4—dc20   AC

CONTENTS

WORLD EXPLORERS

THE EARLY EXPLORERS

THE FIRST GREAT AGE OF DISCOVERY

THE SECOND GREAT AGE OF DISCOVERY

THE THIRD GREAT AGE OF DISCOVERY

CHELSEA HOUSE PUBLISHERS

Into the Unknown

Michael Collins

It is difficult to define most eras in history with any precision, but not so the space age. On October 4, 1957, it burst on us with little warning when the Soviet Union launched *Sputnik*, a 184-pound cannonball that circled the globe once every 96 minutes. Less than 4 years later, the Soviets followed this first primitive satellite with the flight of Yuri Gagarin, a 27-year-old fighter pilot who became the first human to orbit the earth. The Soviet Union's success prompted President John F. Kennedy to decide that the United States should "land a man on the moon and return him safely to earth" before the end of the 1960s. We now had not only a space age but a space race.

I was born in 1930, exactly the right time to allow me to participate in Project Apollo, as the U.S. lunar program came to be known. As a young man growing up, I often found myself too young to do the things I wanted—or suddenly too old, as if someone had turned a switch at midnight. But for Apollo, 1930 was the perfect year to be born, and I was very lucky. In 1966 I enjoyed circling the earth for three days, and in 1969 I flew to the moon and laughed at the sight of the tiny earth, which I could cover with my thumbnail.

How the early explorers would have loved the view from space! With one glance Christopher Columbus could have plotted his course and reassured his crew that the world was indeed round. In 90 minutes Magellan could have looked down at every port of call in the *Victoria's* three-year circumnavigation of the globe. Given a chance to map their route from orbit, Lewis and Clark could have told President Jefferson that there was no easy Northwest Passage but that a continent of exquisite diversity awaited their scrutiny.

In a physical sense, we have already gone to most places that we can. That is not to say that there are not new adventures awaiting us deep in the sea or on the red plains of Mars, but more important than reaching new places will be understanding those we have already visited. There are vital gaps in our understanding of how our planet works as an ecosystem and how our planet fits into the infinite order of the universe. The next great age may well be the age of assimilation, in which we use microscope and telescope to evaluate what we have discovered and put that knowledge to use. The adventure of being first to reach may be replaced by the satisfaction of being first to grasp. Surely that is a form of exploration as vital to our well-being, and perhaps even survival, as the distinction of being the first to explore a specific geographical area.

The explorers whose stories are told in the books of this series did not just sail perilous seas, scale rugged mountains, traverse blistering deserts, dive to the depths of the ocean, or land on the moon. Their voyages and expeditions were journeys of mind as much as of time and distance, through which they—and all of mankind—were able to reach a greater understanding of our universe. That challenge remains, for all of us. The imperative is to see, to understand, to develop knowledge that others can use, to help nurture this planet that sustains us all. Perhaps being born in 1975 will be as lucky for a new generation of explorer as being born in 1930 was for Neil Armstrong, Buzz Aldrin, and Mike Collins.

The Reader's Journey

William H. Goetzmann

This volume is one of a series that takes us with the great explorers of the ages on bold journeys over the oceans and the continents and into outer space. As we travel along with these imaginative and courageous journeyers, we share their adventures and their knowledge. We also get a glimpse of that mysterious and inextinguishable fire that burned in the breast of men such as Magellan and Columbus—the fire that has propelled all those throughout the ages who have been driven to leave behind family and friends for a voyage into the unknown.

No one has ever satisfactorily explained the urge to explore, the drive to go to the "back of beyond." It is certain that it has been present in man almost since he began walking erect and first ventured across the African savannas. Sparks from that same fire fueled the transoceanic explorers of the Ice Age, who led their people across the vast plain that formed a land bridge between Asia and North America, and the astronauts and scientists who determined that man must reach the moon.

Besides an element of adventure, all exploration involves an element of mystery. We must not confuse exploration with discovery. Exploration is a purposeful human activity—a search for something. Discovery may be the end result of that search; it may also be an accident, as when Columbus found a whole new world while searching for the Indies. Often, the explorer may not even realize the full significance of what he has discovered, as was the case with Columbus. Exploration, on the other hand, is the product of a cultural or individual curiosity; it is a unique process that has enabled mankind to know and understand the world's oceans, continents, and polar regions. It is at the heart of scientific thinking. One of its most significant aspects is that it teaches people to ask the right questions; by doing so, it forces us to reevaluate what we think we know and understand. Thus knowledge progresses, and we are driven constantly to a new awareness and appreciation of the universe in all its infinite variety.

The motivation for exploration is not always pure. In his fascination with the new, man often forgets that others have been there before him. For example, the popular notion of the discovery of America overlooks the complex Indian civilizations that had existed there for thousands of years before the arrival of Europeans. Man's desire for conquest, riches, and fame is often linked inextricably with his quest for the unknown, but a story that touches so closely on the human essence must of necessity treat war as well as peace, avarice with generosity, both pride and humility, frailty and greatness. The story of exploration is above all a story of humanity and of man's understanding of his place in the universe.

The WORLD EXPLORERS series has been divided into four sections. The first treats the explorers of the ancient world, the Viking explorers of the 9th through the 11th centuries, and Marco Polo and the medieval explorers. The rest of the series is divided into three great ages of exploration. The first is the era of Columbus and Magellan: the period spanning the 15th and 16th centuries, which saw the discovery and exploration of the New World and the world ocean. The second might be called the age of science and imperialism, the era made possible by the scientific advances of the 17th century, which witnessed the discovery of the world's last two undiscovered continents, Australia and Antarctica, the mapping of all the continents and oceans, and the establishment of colonies all over the world. The third great age refers to the most ambitious quests of the 20th century—the probing of space and of the ocean's depths.

As we reach out into the darkness of outer space and other galaxies, we come to better understand how our ancestors confronted *oecumene,* or the vast earthly unknown. We learn once again the meaning of an unknown 18th-century sea captain's advice to navigators:

> And if by chance you make a landfall on the shores of another sea in a far country inhabited by savages and barbarians, remember you this: the greatest danger and the surest hope lies not with fires and arrows but in the quicksilver hearts of men.

At its core, exploration is a series of moral dramas. But it is these dramas, involving new lands, new people, and exotic ecosystems of staggering beauty, that make the explorers' stories not only moral tales but also some of the greatest adventure stories ever recorded. They represent the process of learning in its most expansive and vivid forms. We see that real life, past and present, transcends even the adventures of the starship *Enterprise.*

The Passage to Cathay

Just after dawn on June 24, 1497, the tiny three-masted ship *Mathew* was sailing west through the cold waters of the North Atlantic, as it had been doing since the last day of May, when its Venetian master, John Cabot, had set its course due west from Dursey Head, Ireland. Barely 60 feet long, the *Mathew* employed the typical rigging of the day: a large square sail on each of the fore- and mainmasts, with a fore-and-aft sail on its mizzen. The ship's low waist, between the raised forecastle and quarterdeck, was protected by canvas screens mounted on both sides to keep the crew from being drenched. Despite its seeming flimsiness, the *Mathew* could survive weather that would sink larger ships, and in certain circumstances its smallness was an advantage, for the *Mathew* made up in maneuverability and responsiveness what it lacked in size and possessed a shallow draft ideal for exploring unknown coasts. That morning, Cabot and his crew of 18 were 35 days out of Bristol, England, in search of a new western route to China.

Save for a stiff northerly gale on June 22, the passage of the *Mathew* had thus far gone smoothly. At about five o'clock, a dark, craggy point of land rose out of the sea ahead, 12 to 15 miles in the distance. Cabot immediately named it Prima Vista—the first seen. A few moments later, the *Mathew*'s crew sighted a large island 15 miles to the north of Prima Vista. Their master dubbed it St. John's

Very little is known about the life of John Cabot, seen here in an oil painting by an unknown artist. An observer at the court of King Henry VII of England described him as "a lower-class Venetian, of a fine mind, very expert in navigation."

in honor of the herald of Christ, whose feast day it was.
As the ship neared land, a lower but equally rocky and
forbidding coast appeared just to the north. The prospect
of a dawn landfall pleased the *Mathew*'s company, for the
men would have plenty of time to look for a safe harbor,
taking care to avoid hidden shoals and reefs, but even in
late June the approaches to the isle of St. John (later re-
named by the French Belle Isle) were still choked by ice—
a forbidding prospect for a small wooden craft such as the
Mathew. Cabot therefore turned south to look for an anchorage. His ship skirted the rocky, wave-beaten coast for
three or four miles before reaching a wide inlet, beyond
which opened up what Cabot described to a contemporary
as "good and temperate country" covered with tall pines.
After the *Mathew* anchored, Cabot took a few members
of the crew ashore in the ship's small boat. There, the
men ceremonially raised a crucifix in praise of the Savior,
a banner with the cross of St. George representing England, and a Venetian flag, to honor Cabot's home city,
and took formal possession of the country for King Henry
VII of England, the voyage's sponsor. At noon, Cabot
measured the harbor's latitude: 51 degrees 30 minutes
north latitude, almost precisely due west of Dursey Head.
This measurement was preserved in a letter written in the
winter of 1497–98 by John Day, an English merchant
living in Spain, to Christopher Columbus, who was then
preparing for his third voyage to America, this time in
search of a southern continent reputed to exist as a "balance" to Africa. Columbus, who regarded his discoveries
in the New World as akin to personal property, was most
eager to keep abreast of new maritime developments. Day's
letter places Cabot's anchorage three or four miles south
of Cape Degrat, either in Quirpon Harbor or Griquet
Harbor, on the east coast of the large island known today
as Newfoundland. The latter was most likely the site of
Cabot's landing, since a narrow entrance makes the former
difficult to spot from the sea.

Cabot and Columbus had more in common than a fortuitous landfall in the New World occasioned by their determination to discover a new route to the spices and wealth of the Far East. Like Columbus, Cabot was born in the powerful Italian maritime city of Genoa, probably in the early 1450s. (Columbus was born in 1451.) Although very little about Cabot's life is known, it is certain that as a young man he moved to Venice, Genoa's great economic and seafaring rival, where in 1476 the Venetian senate confirmed him as a citizen of the republic. Venetian documents indicate that he took part in the buying and selling of real estate, but he probably also sailed on trading voyages, for he later told Raimond de Soncino, the Milanese ambassador to London, that he had made a trip to the Islamic holy city of Mecca, on the Arabian peninsula in present-day Saudi Arabia. It is possible that he also visited some of the other cities of the Middle East where

This 16th-century engraving by Theodore de Bry depicts Christopher Columbus and his men landing on the island of Hispaniola. The motivation behind Columbus's first voyage and Cabot's two expeditions was the same—to discover a western route to Asia.

Italian merchants were in the habit of calling in order to trade for the spices brought there by Arab caravans. Europeans prized spices, such as cinnamon, clove, pepper, and nutmeg, as flavor enhancers and food preservatives; other spices were valued for their aromatic or medicinal qualities. The prosperity of Genoa and Venice was essentially based on the spice trade, but the origin of these exotic items remained shrouded in mystery. Cabot's queries apparently revealed to him (erroneously, as it turns out) only that the spices originated somewhere in northeast Asia, probably in the fabulously wealthy realms of Cathay and Cipango, as the 13th-century Venetian traveler Marco

A soulful Marco Polo, the 13th-century traveler, as painted by his fellow Venetian, the great Renaissance artist Titian. Most of Polo's tales of the splendor and might of the East were disbelieved by his fellow citizens, who sarcastically dubbed him Marco Millions, but he was an inspiration to Cabot, Columbus, and countless other adventurers.

Polo had described and named China and Japan.

Although Columbus and Cabot shared similar goals, they utilized slightly different methods. Both mariners believed that one could reach the East by sailing west, across the Ocean Sea (as the Atlantic Ocean was oftentimes referred to in their day) from Europe, but Cabot believed that the quickest way to the spice regions was far north of Columbus's route. Prior to his first voyage, Columbus hoped to reach Cipango by making his westing—finding the desired parallel and holding to it until one's destination is reached—along the same lines of latitude as the Canary Islands. Cabot either believed that Cipango occupied a higher latitude than Columbus had thought or was attempting to reach northern China, for his westing—which he was extremely successful in maintaining—was made from Dursey Head, Ireland, far north of the Canaries. Again like Columbus, Cabot initially sought support for his idea in Portugal and Spain, the two premier European seafaring powers of the time, but the Portuguese were trying to reach the East by sailing around Africa, and the Spanish, flushed with Columbus's success, turned him down.

He met with better luck in England. Because England was at the far end of the trade route from the East, its people paid the highest prices for spices. Its king, Henry VII, had missed out on sponsoring Columbus, whose discovery he enviously described as "a thing more divine than human," so when Cabot—described by the Spanish ambassador as a "man like Columbus"—proposed a western voyage to Henry, the monarch was willing to listen. English merchants were also interested in the proposal, for the development of a direct trade route with Asia meant lower costs and higher profits for themselves. Their support was crucial, for Cabot, in seeking permission to explore under the royal flag, had stated that he would undertake the expedition at his own expense, no doubt hoping—or intending—to obtain corporate sponsorship. In March

1496, King Henry VII granted to "our wel-beloved John Cabot citizen of Venice, to Lewis, Sebastian, and Santus, sonnes of the sayd John . . . full and free authority, leave, and power to sail to all parts, countryes, and seas of the East, of the West, and of the North, under our banners and ensignes . . . to seek out, discover, and finde whatsoever isles, countryes, regions, or provinces of the heathen and infidels . . . which before this time have bene unknowen to all Christians." Cabot received a monopoly on all trade, free from customs duties, provided that the Crown kept title to all discoveries. The king claimed one-fifth of all profits and commanded all English subjects, "as well on land as on sea," to render Cabot all necessary assistance.

But enlightened self-interest, every bit as much as the royal directive, motivated the merchants of Bristol, a port city at the mouth of the Severn River in southwestern England, to aid Cabot. Situated halfway between Iceland and Spain, Bristol was perfectly positioned to profit from the north-south trade in woolens (from the nearby Cotswold region), dried fish (from Iceland), and wine and olive oil (from Spain and Portugal). This commerce had by 1400 made Bristol the second-largest trade center in England, but by the middle of the 15th century its prosperity was being threatened by the rise of the German cities of the Hanseatic League—Hamburg, Bremen, Lübeck, and others—and their increasing dominance of the northern trade. Bristol was therefore keenly interested in new trade routes, and in the decades prior to Cabot's proposal Bristol seamen had set out at least once for the Middle East and on several other occasions in search of new fishing grounds in the Atlantic. Although these missions had been unsuccessful—the Genoese sabotaged the eastern initiative, and the Atlantic refused to yield the whereabouts of Brazil, Antilia, or any of the other reputed islands to the west— the potential return on Cabot's venture seemed worth the risk, and the Bristol merchants provided him with the

Mathew, a crew, and enough provisions to last seven or eight months.

Although preliminary investigation, following his landfall, gave Cabot no reason to believe that he had discovered anything that would repay the Bristol financiers for their confidence, he was nonetheless certain that he had reached the East, according to John Day's letter to Columbus. The contrast with the fabled Orient could not have been more extreme: Instead of the gold-roofed palaces and jewel-encrusted bridges Marco Polo had described, the cautious explorers encountered in the course of their brief reconnaissance only thick forest; the remains of a campfire; a needle; snares for game; a long piece of wood,

The Ottoman Turks lay siege to Constantinople, the seven-hilled city regarded in medieval Europe as the second Rome. Genoa, Venice, and other European commercial centers had long obtained Eastern trade goods, such as spices, in the Levant, but after Constantinople's fall Europeans were forced to more actively seek new trade routes. These changed economic circumstances motivated voyages such as Cabot's.

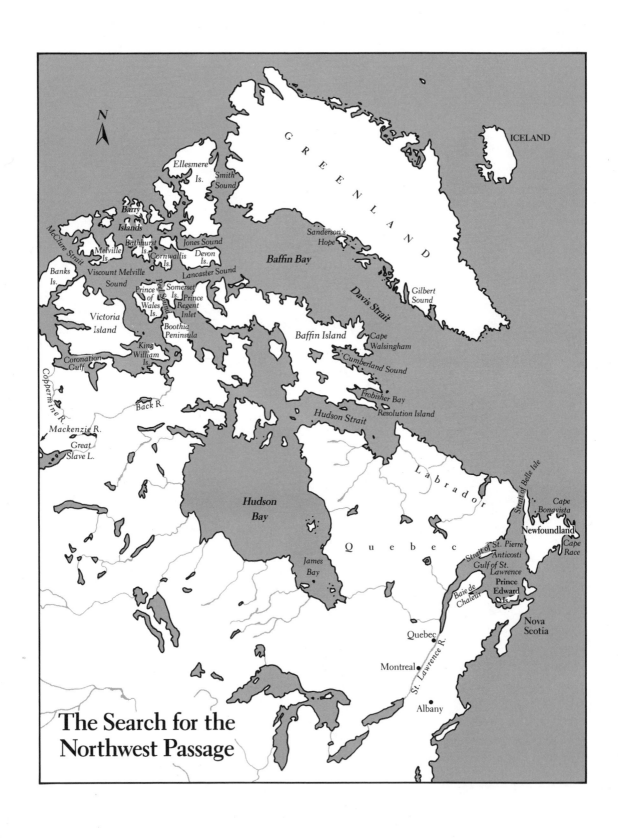

N

ICELAND

G R E E N L A N D

Ellesmere Is.
Smith Sound
Barry Islands
Jones Sound
Bathurst Is.
Melville Is.
Cornwallis Is.
Devon Is.
Sanderson's Hope
McClure Strait
Banks Is.
Viscount Melville Sound
Lancaster Sound
Baffin Bay
Prince of Wales Is.
Somerset Is.
Prince Regent Inlet
Gilbert Sound
Victoria Island
Boothia Peninsula
Davis Strait
King William Is.
Coronation Gulf
Baffin Island
Cape Walsingham
Coppermine R.
Back R.
Cumberland Sound
Mackenzie R.
Great Slave L.
Frobisher Bay
Resolution Island
Hudson Strait
L a b r a d o r
Strait of Bella Isle
Cape Bonavista
Hudson Bay
Newfoundland
Cape Race
Q u e b e c
St. Pierre
Anticosti
Strait of
Gulf of St. Lawrence
James Bay
Prince Edward Is.
Baie de Chaleur
Nova Scotia
Quebec
St. Lawrence R.
Montreal
Albany

The Search for the
Northwest Passage

painted red, with a hole at each end; and animal dung, most likely from caribou or moose. This initial exploration of Newfoundland was extremely brief, for Cabot did not dare move beyond crossbow range (roughly 1,000 feet) of the *Mathew*. After the crew replenished the ship's water supply from a nearby stream, the *Mathew* weighed anchor.

The tiny ship sailed south, past long stretches of rocky coast, dashed rhythmically by the ocean swells. Occasional inlets led into harbors, but fog almost certainly made exploration difficult. A French traveler off the Newfoundland coast in late June 1601 described fogs "which we might perceive to come and wrap us about, holding us continually prisoners three whole days for two days of fair weather that they permitted us." Cabot worked his ship carefully along the coast, successfully avoiding reefs and shoal water, past Fogo Island, around Cape Freels, to Cape Bonavista, where codfish abounded in numbers far exceeding the wildest dreams of Bristol fishermen. The fish swarmed so thickly that Cabot's men could catch them with a weighted basket lowered over the side. Cabot had happened upon the Grand Bank, which remains one of the world's richest fishing areas. At other points, broad meadows ashore gave Cabot the impression of cultivated fields; once, he believed he detected villages. He also saw two large creatures chasing each other, but he could not tell whether they were animals or men.

Finally, after cruising south for about two weeks, the *Mathew* rounded a long point of land with low slate cliffs. On the other side, the coast turned sharply to the west, and the sea extended in that direction and to the south all the way to the horizon and seemingly far beyond. Cabot was convinced that he had found the western sea route to Cathay. From the *Mathew*'s pitching deck, he measured the latitude of the land's southernmost point and found it to be 45 degrees 45 minutes north latitude, as he reported on his return, due west of the mouth of the Gironde River in southwestern France.

The search for the Northwest Passage took place in these wintry regions and frigid waters. Most of these waterways are frozen over throughout the year; even during the brief summer, icebergs make navigation treacherous at best.

The *Mathew* had just rounded Cape Race, the south-eastern corner of Newfoundland. In future centuries, English ships would make Cape Race their goal on transatlantic voyages; as the low cliffs appeared out of the fog, the vessels would fix their location before turning the corner and making for Nova Scotia, Boston, or New York. Considering the tossing platform from which he had to make his observations—latitude was determined by measuring the angle between the North Star and the horizon—Cabot made a fair estimate of his latitude. (Columbus, by contrast, for all his navigational prowess, sometimes made astoundingly inaccurate latitude readings.) Newfoundland's southernmost point, Cape Pine, which is 18 miles west of Cape Race, lies at 46 degrees 37 minutes north latitude. Past Cape Pine and its neighbor to the west, Cape Mary, the coast of Newfoundland bends sharply northward, forming Placentia Bay; the next land to the west, Burin Peninsula, is low and generally invisible from Cape Mary. A deep ocean trough extends through Placentia Bay, meaning, according to naval historian Samuel Eliot Morison, that if Cabot did enter the bay and take soundings, he would have found no bottom, further convincing him that he had entered open ocean.

Having apparently found the passage, Cabot decided to return home, probably in order to prepare a more ambitious expedition. The *Mathew* doubled Cape Race and headed north, hugging the shore all the way. The weather must have improved, for John Day reported that most of the coastline was visible on the return journey, and the crew sighted two islands that had presumably been hidden by fog before. Cabot promised one to a Burgundian companion on board and the other to the Genoese barber he had brought along. In the last days of July, about a month after having first sighted land, the *Mathew* rounded Cape Degrat and headed eastward out to sea.

Apparently, the seeming discovery of a northwest passage to China had not convinced the crew of the *Mathew* of its master's abilities, for they now insisted that he steer a slightly southern course rather than simply keeping his easting. For unknown reasons, Cabot agreed—Day recorded that the crew "confused" him. Favorable winds hastened *Mathew*'s return passage, but when land was sighted after the remarkably short period of 15 days, it proved to be Brittany, on the coast of France, not Ireland or England. Cabot then took his ship due north for 100 miles, rounded Land's End, England's westernmost tip, and entered the Severn River, anchoring his vessel off Bristol on August 6, 1497.

The waterfront in Bristol, the city in southwest England from where Cabot departed on his two northwest voyages. The cathedral there, whose spire can be seen looming in the background was completed in 1142.

Cabot's sponsor, Henry VII of England, won his throne by returning from exile in Britanny to defeat Richard III at the Battle of Bosworth Field. His subsequent marriage to Elizabeth, daughter of Edward IV, united the feuding houses of York and Lancaster, put an end to the destructive dynastic quarrels known as the Wars of the Roses, and began the Tudor dynasty.

The skepticism of the Bristol merchants about Cabot's claims may have hastened his departure for London—he had brought back no treasure that indicated he had reached the Orient—but in any event he wasted little time before carrying his story to King Henry. He no doubt took some of his crew with him; Raimond de Soncino reported that the English would not have believed the Venetian's report if his Bristol crew had not testified to its truth. Henry VII welcomed the good news. The books for the royal household show that on August 11 the king, not noted for his generosity, granted Cabot a gift of 10 pounds sterling, a healthy sum for the time. Four months later Cabot was awarded a pension of 20 pounds per year.

Cabot believed that he had found the eastern tip of Asia. Soncino told his prince that "his Majesty [Henry VII] has won a part of Asia without a stroke of the sword." Two maps drawn just after Cabot's voyage, the Contarini-Roselli world map of 1506 and the Ruysch map of 1508, both place Cabot's discovery at the northeastern edge of the Eurasian continent, far to the east and just north of Cathay. Cabot evidently described the Avalon Peninsula, as the southeasternmost portion of Newfoundland is now known, as an island, for King Henry referred to Cabot as "hym that founde the new Isle." Other references to Cabot's discovery were less explicit; it was called simply the "New Found Land." Cabot proposed to clear up these ambiguities by undertaking a second voyage of exploration, in the course of which he intended to venture farther west, constantly hugging the shore, until he came, according to Soncino, "to an island which he calls Cipango . . . where he thinks all the spices of the world have their origin." He planned to found a trading colony there, which would turn London into "a more important mart for Spices than Alexandria." This scheme impressed the king, whose support in turn dispelled the skepticism of the Bristol merchants. With the help of their London counterparts, the Bristol business community outfitted four ships for Cabot;

the king, as he had promised, provided one more. The fleet was laden with a year's worth of provisions and goods deemed suitable for trade with the Chinese for spices—"cloth, Caps, Laces, points and other trifles."

While preparations were ongoing, Cabot, back in Bristol, conducted himself in a manner he believed to be consistent with his newfound celebrity. He assumed the title of grand admiral and used his stipend from the king to dress himself in silk finery. The Venetian merchant Pasqualigo wrote to his brothers in August 1497 that "the English run after him like mad people, so that he can enlist as many of them as he pleases, and a number of our own rogues besides." Cabot's Burgundian companion and the Genoese barber, both now owners of islands, styled themselves counts, and a couple of poor Italian monks sought to accompany the return trip in the hope of being named bishops. Still sure of themselves, despite their recent miscalculation, the *Mathew*'s crew claimed that the second voyage would take no more than 15 days. The fleet departed from Bristol at the end of May 1498, with Cabot's supporters confidently expecting him to return in August or September with word of riches for all.

News of Cabot's expedition was forthcoming only in the negative, however. Months passed with no word from the fleet. Although it is likely that one of Cabot's ships returned to England, there is no record of the fate of the other four. It is as if Cabot sailed over the horizon and off the edge of the earth, as superstitious sailors once believed might happen to those who ventured too far in unknown waters. The 16th-century historian Polidoro Vergilio had a more commonsense explanation of the Venetian's fate: "Cabot found his new lands only in the ocean's bottom, to which he and his ship are thought to have sunk, since . . . he was never heard of more." But his dream remained afloat, and for centuries to come individuals and nations would tempt fate and seek to outdo one another in the search for the Northwest Passage.

DOS LIBROS
DE COSMOGRAPHIA

Compuestos nueuamente por Hiero-
nymo Giraua Tarragones.

CON EL TIEMPO
GIRAVA

The French Effort

After Cabot's disappearance, England's concern with its New Found Land faded, and it left the region to the European fishermen who flocked there. Only Cabot's oldest son, Sebastian, seemed interested in carrying on his work. In 1508, he allegedly took two ships across the Atlantic at an even higher latitude than his father had sailed, but upon his return his report—he claimed to have reached what is today known as the Hudson Strait—was dismissed, for the younger Cabot had earned something of a reputation as a boastful and foolish fellow. For strategic reasons, England needed to maintain the friendship of Spain, which claimed control over the western sea routes by virtue of Columbus's discoveries, and so for the time being the English search for the Northwest Passage halted. But for other European nations, seafaring exploration had taken on an increased importance. In 1498, almost 70 years of Portuguese efforts had culminated in the success of Vasco da Gama's expedition to India, made by the eastern route around the Cape of Good Hope at the southern tip of Africa. In its immediate ramifications, da Gama's discovery was even more momentous than Columbus's. At last, the dream of a direct link to the Indies had been fulfilled, and in the following decades Portugal became the center of the new Eastern commerce that bypassed the costly and difficult Mediterranean routes. Within six years of da Gama's voyage, spices sold in Lisbon for one-fifth as much

In this engraving from the title page of a mid-16th-century atlas, a medieval cosmographer points to the "littus incognitum," or unknown shore, believed to lie to the west between Europe and Asia.

as they did in Venice. Ports in Italy and southern France lost most of their trade to Portugal and fell into decline, and the balance of power began shifting inexorably from those states that controlled the Mediterranean to those that controlled the ocean.

On the first day of the new year 1515, Francis, duke of Angoulême, acceded to the throne of France. A lover of all things Italian, the new king brought Italian artists and scholars, including Leonardo da Vinci, to his court, and under his rule colonies of Italian merchants and financiers enjoyed complete freedom to pursue profits and boost the French economy. One such group, from Florence, had its headquarters in Lyons, a city on the Rhône River in east-central France; among its number was a gentleman trader and accomplished mariner named Giovanni da Verrazano. Having inherited the merchant profession from his father, the wellborn Verrazano had traveled widely throughout the Mediterranean world, living for a time in Egypt and Syria and devoting himself to learning the mariner's art. He became, in the words of the historian Lawrence Wroth, "a well educated, imaginative, and aggressive seaman." Exploration intrigued Verrazano, and there is evidence that he accompanied a French expedition to Newfoundland in 1508, when he was 23 years old. He was also friendly with the Portuguese explorer Ferdinand Magellan, who in 1519, under the flag of Charles I of Spain, Francis's great rival, set sail in an attempt to find a strait through South America to the Pacific. (The Pacific had been discovered by Europeans in 1513, when the Spanish explorer Vasco Núñez de Balboa crossed the Isthmus of Panama and reached its shores, although it received its name from Magellan on his epic voyage.)

The Portuguese success in reaching the East had devastated the silk trade on which Verrazano and his colleagues depended, making the discovery of an alternate route to the Far East vital. When the 18 survivors of

Portuguese mariner Vasco da Gama reached India in 1498 by rounding the Cape of Good Hope. At the time it was the longest sea voyage ever completed, and it helped shift the center of power in Europe from the Mediterranean to the Atlantic seaboard. On subsequent missions, da Gama demonstrated an exceptional capacity for cruelty, but he succeeded in giving Portugal the first European empire in Asia.

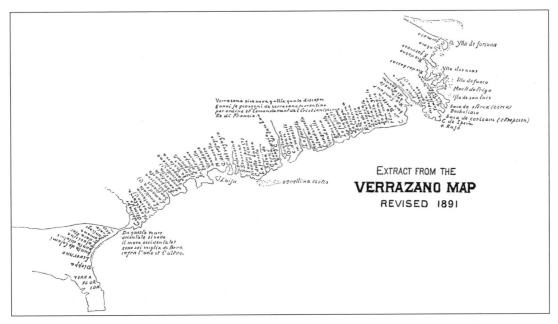

EXTRACT FROM THE
VERRAZANO MAP
REVISED 1891

Magellan's attempt to circumnavigate the globe—Magellan was not among them, having perished in the Philippines—returned to Spain in 1522, they reported that distance, frequent storms, and treacherous navigation made the route they had discovered, through the Strait of Magellan, impractical as a commercial channel. Although Spanish exploration had revealed much of the New World, no one was completely certain yet what lay between Florida and Newfoundland. Verrazano believed that the passage to Cathay was to be found in the mid-Atlantic latitudes and proposed to lead an expedition to prove as much. His merchant compatriots agreed and formed a company to finance the voyage. Royal support was also forthcoming, for King Francis, who begrudged Charles of Spain success in any venture, was intensely envious of the Spanish crown's overseas claims and hoped to solve France's traditional financial woes—which were aggravated by his constant wars —through successful maritime exploration.

The king gave Verrazano a caravel (a small three-masted

A slightly modified detail from the map of the eastern coast of North America drawn by Girolamo da Verrazano, brother of the explorer, in 1529. Despite Giovanni da Verrazano's error in believing that the Pacific Ocean divided North America almost in two and was separated from the Atlantic only by a narrow isthmus—represented here as a slender strip of land just above Florida—he did succeed in proving North America to be a separate continent.

sailing ship ideally suited for voyages of exploration) from the French navy, and the Lyons company furnished three more vessels. The fleet left the harbor of Dieppe on New Year's Day, 1524, only to meet a violent storm that sank two ships and drove the others back to port. Reduced by half, early on its second voyage Verrazano's fleet encountered several Spanish merchant ships while off the coast of Spain. France and Spain were again at war, so Verrazano took several of the Spanish vessels captive and dispatched them back to France under the watchful eyes of the officers and crew of *La Normande*, leaving himself and 50 men in the 100-ton caravel *La Dauphine* to complete his mission.

Sailing alone across the Atlantic was generally not considered prudent seamanship—Columbus, for example, was always hesitant about sailing without accompaniment—for another ship could prove useful in case of mishap, but Verrazano was an exceptionally self-confident and hard-driving commander. (In his official account of the voyage, written in the form of a letter to Francis I, Verrazano mentions no other individual by name and refers to his crew repeatedly as *la turba marittima*—the maritime mob.) In mid-March, after surviving a storm even more violent than the one that had sunk its sister ships, *La Dauphine* came upon a low-lying coast that, as the ship drew nearer, resolved itself into sandy beaches with wide, rolling dunes. Verrazano recorded his latitude as 34 degrees north, "like Carthage and Damascus"; this and his description of the coast place his landfall just south of modern-day Cape Fear, North Carolina. Huge fires burning on the beaches revealed the country to be inhabited.

Verrazano took *La Dauphine* southward along the coast to look for a harbor. After searching for about 100 miles without success, he ordered the ship put about, as he later wrote, "so as not to meet with the Spaniards," whose presence in the New World extended southward from Florida. After anchoring *La Dauphine* in the open sea at the site of its first landfall, Verrazano sent the ship's boat ashore. As the landing party approached the shore, they saw human figures retreating in fear, but when the Frenchmen gestured friendlily, the natives rushed forward in delight and made signs to show where the boat might best land. Verrazano described the people as "dark in color . . . with thick black hair, not very long, tied back beyond the head like a small tail. They go completely naked except that around their loins they wear skins of small animals. . . . From what we could tell . . . they resembled the Orientals." The natives marveled over the white men and their strange clothes and offered them food.

Moving farther inland, the party encountered beautiful fields and forests, full of palm trees, cypresses, laurels, and other arboreal specimens the French had never seen before. A sweet smell wafted from the woods; ever on the lookout for profits for his backers, Verrazano decided that he had found a source of narcotic liquors. Animals and birds abounded, making the region perfect, in Verrazano's mind, for royal hunts.

Under cloudless skies, Verrazano and his men returned to their ship and set sail to the north, following the eastward-trending shoreline. After several days sail up the North Carolina coast, Verrazano was delighted to find the land dwindling to a narrow isthmus, scarcely a mile across, with open ocean on the other side. He wrote later that "we could see the eastern sea [the Pacific] from the ship." Convinced that his route to Cathay lay just over this barrier, Verrazano searched with increasing frustration for an entrance. The search proved futile; the isthmus widened, and the ocean disappeared. What Verrazano had seen was the Outer Banks off Cape Hatteras, North Carolina, which form a barrier dividing Pamlico Sound from the Atlantic Ocean. It would be years, however, before a more accurate picture of the geography of this region emerged, and many cartographers, including Verrazano's brother Girolamo,

Giovanni da Verrazano was most likely a member of the lesser Tuscan nobility. It has long been believed that Verrazano was born in the family castle in the Chianti region in Greve, some 30 miles south of Florence, sometime around 1480, although some scholars have recently suggested that he was born in Lyons, France, which was home to a large Florentine community.

who was aboard *La Dauphine*, and Robertus de Bailly, the creator of the famous Bailly globe of 1530, were to draw North America as Verrazano envisioned it—as two nearly separate land masses, falling away far to the west, linked only by a tiny isthmus that separated the Atlantic and its western counterpart, the "Sea of Verrazano."

Frustrated in their hopes, *La Dauphine*'s company continued north. Sailing by day, anchoring at night, occasionally exploring on shore, the adventurers beheld a land covered almost entirely with thick forests. At one point, the Frenchmen seized a young native boy from his mother to take back with them to France. The explorers missed Chesapeake Bay; dangerous shoals in that region most likely forced them too far out to sea to notice the entrance.

On April 17, sailing before a soft southwest wind, *La Dauphine* came upon "a very agreeable place between two small but prominent hills; between them a very wide river . . . flowed out into the sea." Not trusting the unknown passage, Verrazano decided to anchor off the coast. He and several members of his crew then clambered into the

This mid-16th-century map of the Americas illustrates some of the mistaken notions of geography prevalent in the years following Verrazano's voyage. Note the narrow isthmus separating the Atlantic from the Pacific and connecting the northeastern regions (labeled Francisca) claimed by France and the remainder of the continent; notice as well that the cartographer has placed Asia (India, Cathay, and Zipangri) just to the west of North America.

ship's boat and rowed up the river mouth. A beautiful, densely wooded land opened up before them. With his mercantile sensibility, Verrazano immediately speculated that the hills on either side of the river would yield precious metals. Suddenly, a lookout spotted natives ashore. Brightly dressed in multicolored bird feathers, the Indians rushed joyfully toward the newcomers and gestured for them to land. Evidently not trusting the native inhabitants, the French continued onward for another mile before the river, as Verrazano put it, "formed a beautiful lake, about three leagues [about eight miles] in circumference." Thirty canoes full of natives darted across the lake toward the Europeans, but without warning a violent squall blew up, forcing Verrazano to return to his ship, "leaving the land with much regret on account of its favorable conditions."

This incident marks the European discovery of New York Bay. Verrazano anchored *La Dauphine* off the entrance to the Narrows; the two hills he referred to were either the Navesink Highlands of Staten Island or Brooklyn Heights, and the "lake" was most likely the Upper Bay. As he hoisted sail to move on, Verrazano complimented his king by naming this beautiful region Angoulême.

Verrazano then took *La Dauphine* northeastward, keeping within sight of the coast at all times. A large, triangular land body that he came upon—probably Block Island— reminded Verrazano of the Mediterranean island of Rhodes; a century later, English colonials assumed that he had been referring to Aquidneck Island, in Narragansett Bay, and named the colony that surrounded it Rhode Island. Verrazano did anchor his ship in the bay for 15 days, which afforded the crew their first opportunity for shore leave on the entire trip. The friendly inhabitants of the region, whom Verrazano described as "the most beautiful and [having] the most civil customs that we have found on this voyage," proved eager to trade and entertained the sailors with dancing and games.

"Having filled all needs," *La Dauphine* left Narragansett

Bay on May 6. Verrazano successfully navigated dangerous sandbanks east of Nantucket Island, tartly naming
them Armellini after a hated papal tax collector. Cape Cod
received his admiration as an "eminent promontory." Several days later, *La Dauphine* came to a high, mountainous
country, covered with pine and cypress forests. Somewhere
near Casco Bay, Maine, the Frenchmen had a brief fight
with unfriendly Abenaki Indians—described by Verrazano
as "of such crudity and evil manners, so barbarous, that
despite all the signs we could make, we could never con-
verse with them"—with the result that he named the entire
Maine coast the Land of Bad People. Toward the end of
June, *La Dauphine*'s company reached Newfoundland.
By this time, the ship's provisions were nearly exhausted,
so Verrazano decided to take on wood and water and return
to France. A swift passage brought the voyagers safely into
the harbor at Dieppe on July 8, 1524.

Verrazano trumpeted the potential of the new world he
had explored to all who would listen. His journey had
disabused him of the notion that it was part of Asia; he
had demonstrated all but conclusively that what lay to the
west, between Newfoundland and Florida, was a new land,
"unknown to the ancients," and immediately set about
preparing for a return trip. But while Verrazano was away,
France's war with Spain had escalated, and in his need to
devote his resources to battle, King Francis was unable to
provide Verrazano with the ships that he needed. The
Florentine sought support elsewhere, with little success.
He was able to mount two voyages to Brazil, which combined a continued search for a strait through the Americas
with the gathering of timber, but the latter South American
expedition, conducted in 1528, was his last: As his brother
and crew watched helplessly from a longboat offshore,
Verrazano was killed and eaten by cannibals on the beach
of a Caribbean island, most likely Guadeloupe.

Despite his unhappy end, Verrazano's significance to
the history of exploration was immense. Although France

failed to act on Verrazano's greatest ambition, which was to people the rich coastline between Florida and New-foundland with French colonists, his glowing reports about North America did alert the French government to the potential of future colonial development. More important in terms of this story was Verrazano's failure to find a passage to the "happy shores of Cathay." His inability to do so meant that future French and English explorers would again turn their attention to the icy regions of the north in their desire to find a northwest passage to the East that would enable their nations to compete with Portugal, Spain, and later the Netherlands.

Shipbuilders at work; a 16th-century engraving. The hull of a vessel was usually constructed on a slip, from which it could be easily launched. A ship's rigging and masts were added after launching. Oak was the preferred wood for keels; pine was used for side planking and decks, spruce for masts and yards.

Jacques Cartier, whose explorations in the New World provided France with the basis of a North American empire, was born in the Breton port of Saint-Malo in 1491. Even prior to his first voyage in search of the Northwest Passage, he had attained the title of master pilot, which in 15th-century France required as much time and training as a doctorate from a university.

Unfortunately for Francis, Verrazano's explorations did little to fill the royal coffers, but the king remained hopeful that exploration would uncover an easy route to wealth. When, while on a pilgrimage to the 8th-century Benedictine abbey of Mont-Saint-Michel in Brittany in 1532, Francis heard that a local sailor named Jacques Cartier had hopes of finding a passage to Cathay, he lent his support.

Cartier came from a respectable seagoing family in the

ancient, walled Breton port of Saint-Malo, whose fishermen had for some time been visiting the Grand Bank. A
veteran of voyages to Newfoundland and Brazil, Cartier
had attained the rank of master pilot and enjoyed a reputation among mariners as a solid navigator, an excellent
commander, and a just leader of men. He proposed to
find the Northwest Passage to Cathay in the one known
region left unexplored by Cabot and Verrazano: the waters
west of Newfoundland through the Strait of Belle Isle.
After being sworn into the king's service by the vice admiral
of France, Cartier and his company of 61 set sail from
Saint-Malo in two 60-ton caravels on April 20, 1534.

The voyagers were blessed with fair weather; after a fast
passage the two ships raised Cape Bonavista, Newfoundland, on May 10. On July 9, after having spent a month
in harbor waiting out ice and bad weather, the two French
ships penetrated the Strait of Belle Isle and proceeded
westward along the rocky southern coast of Labrador,
through opaque waters studded with small islands and
hidden reefs, before turning south and sailing down the
western coast of Newfoundland. In the journal that he
kept, Cartier vented his disappointment with the landscape, which he described as a region of "stones and wilde
cragges, and a place fit for wilde beasts . . . there is nothing
else but moss and small thorns scattered here and there,
withered and dry. To be short, I believe that this was the
land that God allotted to Cain." He found little of interest
along Newfoundland's western coast, save for great schools
of codfish. On June 24, he sighted the island's southern
tip, Cape Anguille, through a storm. The next day, still
under dark and stormy skies, he set his course west-south-
west to seek the passage.

At first he encountered only islands—the Ile de Bryon,
which Cartier named after a noble supporter in France,
and the Magdalen Islands. Then, on June 30, a low coast
with sandy beaches, meadows of waving grass, and stands
of handsome trees appeared in the distance. The French

carried out several brief landings along the beautiful coast of what would later be known as Prince Edward Island before a squall forced them back out to open water. After crossing the entrance to Northumberland Strait, the ships continued northward. On July 3, the Cartier expedition rounded a promontory and discovered an apparently unlimited expanse of water stretching due west, bordered on the north by hilly, forested country. The strait, for so Cartier judged it to be, appeared both broad and deep. Dozens of the inhabitants of the region—the Micmac Indians—rowed out in canoes from the southern shore to see the strangers. The sailors enhanced their pay by trading with the Indians and looked on with delight as the native women sold them the furs they were wearing, retiring completely naked.

On July 8, Cartier began exploring the bay, which he had named the Baie de Chaleur (Bay of Heat) because of its warm climate. At midday on July 10, after having rowed about 65 miles to the west in their ships' boats, Cartier and his men "had cognizance of the end of said bay, which gave us grief and displeasure." The disappointed party returned to the ships and on July 12 carried on their search to the north.

Bad weather made progress difficult. On July 16 the Frenchmen took refuge in Gaspé Bay, a long inlet that juts westward into the coast. There, they met a party of 200 natives, members of the Huron tribe out on a fishing trip. For more than a week, the explorers mingled and traded with the Huron, coming to understand that the natives came from a city to the west called Canada. (Cartier probably misunderstood the Huron word *cannatta*, which means "village" or "settlement.") On July 24, Cartier ordered his men to erect a 30-foot cross ashore, inscribed with the words *Vive Le Roy de France* (Long Live the King of France). The Indians watched with interest as the French knelt, gave thanks to God, and then used sign language in an attempt to communicate the doctrine of

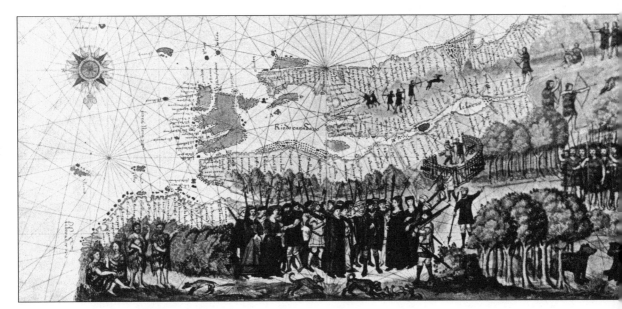

the Resurrection. When the Huron chief Donnaconna protested that the French had raised the cross without his permission, Cartier reassured him that it stood only to guide him on his return. Placated, the chief agreed to allow Cartier to take his two adolescent sons to France, after first extracting a promise that they would be brought back to him.

The French ships made sail and stood to the east the next day. After sailing about 50 miles, the Frenchmen sighted Anticosti Island, which Cartier believed to be part of the mainland. Once the ships rounded a point that Cartier named Cap St. Louis (now East Cape), open water stretched out before them to the northwest. Cartier named this passage the Strait of St. Pierre and gave orders to enter it, but headwinds and strong currents made progress difficult. Stymied, on August 1, Cartier summoned "all our Captains, Masters, and Mariners, to have their advice and opinion" on the next step. (By all accounts, Cartier was much more inclined to such democratic parleys than the more autocratic Verrazano.) The officers and crew voted unanimously to return to France rather than spend the

This 1547 map by a Portuguese cartographer depicts Cartier's arrival in North America. The map is oriented differently than is usual today; south is at top.

winter in a strange land. The next day, the ships put about. After a smooth passage, the little fleet arrived in Saint-Malo on September 5, about four and a half months after it had left.

Although Cartier had not discovered the route to Cathay, he was positive that he still knew where to look for it. With his crew spreading tales of plentiful food and friendly natives, he had no trouble recruiting men for a second voyage. On October 30, 1534, Bryon, Cartier's supporter and the grand admiral of France, issued orders for 3 ships from the French navy to be provisioned for a journey of 15 months' duration and placed at Cartier's disposal. The largest, *La Grande Hermine* (The Great Weasel), carried 12 guns and had a cargo capacity of 120 tons. (In this case, *ton* is not a measurement of weight but a unit of volume equivalent to a double hogshead—a large barrel—of wine.) *La Petite Hermine* (The Small Weasel), at 60 tons and with 8 guns, was smaller. *L'Emerillon* (The Sparrow Hawk) was the smallest of the trio, at 40 tons and with 2 guns, but it made up in maneuverability what it lacked in size. A ship of the kind the English called a pinnace, it was narrower than the other two and was equipped with long oars as well as sails. Similar vessels were used by the Breton fishermen for their voyages to the Grand Bank. The 112-member crew was made up almost exclusively of local salts, at least a dozen of them Cartier's relatives; with them when the ship set sail from Saint-Malo on May 19 were the two Huron lads.

Rough weather hindered the outward passage, and on August 10, three days after its entrance into the Strait of St. Pierre, a gale forced the fleet into the shelter of a bay on the coast of the mainland north of Anticosti Island. As that day was remembered by Catholics as the feast day of Saint Lawrence, the 3rd-century martyr who was roasted alive over a gridiron, Cartier named his refuge the Gulf of St. Lawrence. Over the ensuing centuries, the name gradually came to refer to the entire body of water west of Newfoundland.

When the storm passed, the fleet continued through St. Pierre Strait and past the western tip of Anticosti, which Cartier was now able to identify as an island. As the ships sailed westward, the Huron boys told Cartier that he was entering the wealthy kingdom of Saguenay, a land rich in precious metals, and spoke further of a great river to the west that led to Canada and the fabulous city of Hochelaga. According to the young Indians, this river flowed so far to the west that no man had reached its end. This was precisely what Cartier wanted to hear.

On August 24, the three ships entered the mouth of what Cartier referred to as La Grande Rivière (The Great River) but what his successors would also name the St. Lawrence. Deep and broad, the waterway coursed between high, stony hills, over dangerous shoals, and through several small groups of islands, demanding consummate seamanship from Cartier in order to maneuver his ships successfully upstream against the swift current. On September 7, the fleet halted between a large, richly wooded island and the river's north shore, and his guides informed him that he had entered the province of Canada. Cartier went ashore and exchanged gifts with a party of natives camped on the island. The next day, his old friend Donnaconna appeared with a suite of warriors in 12 canoes to welcome back his sons.

Working their ships carefully upriver, a short distance past the island Cartier and his party came upon a high, majestic stone promontory, thrusting toward them between the Great River and a tributary to the north. At its foot, near the shore, nestled a small Indian settlement that the Huron called Stadacona. In later years, this promontory, at the meeting of the St. Lawrence and the St. Charles rivers, would become famous as the Rock of Quebec.

On September 19, Cartier set sail farther upriver in the tiny *L'Emerillon*, towing the other ships' boats behind, in search of the city of Hochelaga. Currents made progress difficult, and many times *L'Emerillon*'s crew had to man the oars to keep the tiny ship from grounding in rapids or narrow channels. As it struggled upstream, covering 73 miles in 9 days, the pinnace passed wooded shores covered with wild grapes and met friendly Huron who came out to trade. On September 28, the river suddenly widened, forming a long lake, 20 miles in length, that Cartier named Lac Saint-Pierre. Five channels led out of the lake to the southwest; a Huron muskrat-hunting party advised Cartier which one to take. Cartier left *L'Emerillon* anchored at the west end of the lake and continued on with the boats. On October 2 the explorers came to a widening in the river that surrounded a small island. From the north shore, more than 1,000 Hurons rowed out to greet them, throwing cornbread into the boats and bringing children for Cartier to touch as he landed. The next day, Huron guides led Cartier, dressed in his formal cloak, 4 gentlemen volunteers, and 20 sailors armed with pikes through groves of oak trees and open cornfields until they came to a small village fortified by a wooden wall—the city of Hochelaga.

A beaver pool in New France, most likely somewhere along the St. Lawrence River. The French who followed Cartier to Canada never found a great deal of the gold and minerals the Indians spoke of, but they discovered another source of riches in the profusion of fur-bearing animals, especially beavers, living there.

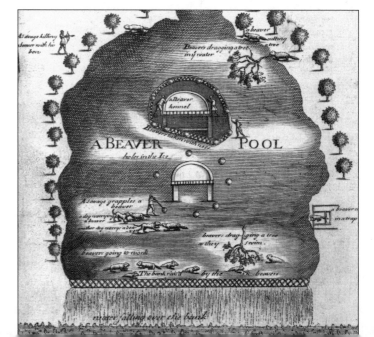

A large hill towered over the little town. Cartier named it Mont Royal, which would survive as the name of the great city that the French would build on the site—Montreal. The Huron led him up the slope. At the top was a stunning vista: the Laurentian Mountains spread out to the north, the Adirondacks and Green Mountains to the south, and the silver ribbon of the St. Lawrence flowing from west to east. To his despair, Cartier also saw just upstream from Hochelaga a great stretch of rapids, "the most impetuous one could possibly see," that rendered further navigation impossible.

Cartier decided to return immediately downriver. In *L'Emerillon*, he arrived at the Rock of Quebec on October 11 and decided soon thereafter that all his ships and crew would spend the winter there. The French were now 1,000 miles from the Atlantic; Cartier recognized that it was unlikely they would be able to reach home before winter set in. The next weeks were spent constructing a fortress on the riverbank; Cartier also occupied himself with re- cording the customs of the Huron, being especially inter- ested in their use of tobacco, which was largely unknown to the Europeans; their gambling; and their liberated sexual practices. He continued to marvel at the profusion of fish and game in and along the St. Lawrence, but this abun- dance was of little help to the Europeans once the icy winter set in. The river froze solid, and four feet of snow covered the shores. Lacking vitamin C in their diet, the French fell victim to scurvy, which causes the gums to bleed and then rot, teeth to fall out, and joints to ache and swell. Twenty-five men died; by mid-February, ac- cording to Cartier, "out of the 110 men that we were, not 10 were well enough to help the others, a thing pitiful to see." All the Frenchmen would surely have perished had not the Huron, in answer to Cartier's prayers, as he in- terpreted it, shown them the healing properties of a potion made from the bark of the annedda tree. Although the first to taste it pronounced it vile, a restored measure of

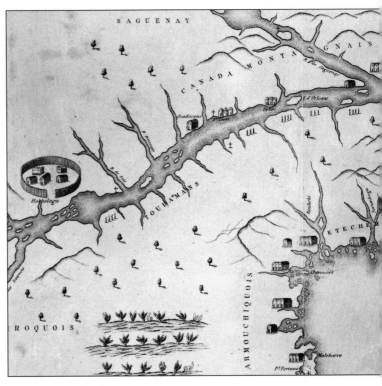

health was apparent within a couple of days.

A relieved Cartier turned his attentions to Donnaconna's increasingly elaborate variations on the theme of the kingdom of Saguenay, which the chief had now transformed into a fabulous realm where white men wore wool clothes and carried huge quantities of gold and rubies. When the spring thaw arrived, Cartier rewarded the chief for his entertainment by kidnapping him, in the belief that the Huron would make a convincing witness to present to King Francis. On May 6, 1536, the remaining 85 men hoisted sail on *La Grande Hermine* and *L'Emerillon*, abandoning *La Petite Hermine*. Some 10 weeks later, the spires of Saint-Malo welcomed the weary travelers home.

Donnaconna proved to be a great success at the French court, where his tales convinced the king that Saguenay could be a source of wealth for France equal to that which

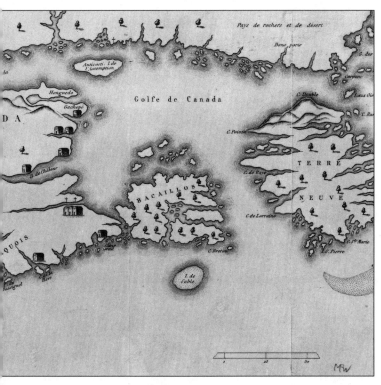

This map of France's discoveries along and around Cartier's Great River was probably drawn not long after his voyages there. The Indian settlement of Hochelaga is represented at left as five dwellings surrounded by a wooden stockade. Cartier's Baie de Chaleur is the large inlet on the southwest coast of the body of water labeled Golfe de Canada but known today as the Gulf of St. Lawrence.

Spain and Portugal had reaped from their overseas ventures. Cartier was ordered to prepare a colonizing expedition; this time, no mention was made of a passage to Cathay. The mission, undertaken in May 1541, failed. Saguenay remained elusive, the winter was again brutal, and Indians attacked the settlement Cartier founded downriver from the Rock of Quebec. In the spring of 1542, Cartier abandoned the first French attempt to settle in the New World. His failure marked the end, for six decades, of the French effort to colonize America as well as of French attempts to find the Northwest Passage. Francis I died in 1547; his successor, Henry II, cared little for exploration. Religious wars arising from the Protestant Reformation came to occupy most of the French crown's energy and money, forcing France to leave the search for the Northwest Passage to others.

QVI·MALE·PENSE

POSVI | TOREM
DEVM | MEVM
ADIV

England in the Arctic

On June 8, 1576, three small ships moved down the Thames River under the noonday sun. The 30-ton *Gabriel* led, followed by the smaller *Michael*. A tiny pinnace brought up the rear. Aboard the *Gabriel*, a dour, bearded man with piercing dark eyes and short black hair watched as the battlements of Greenwich Castle came into view on the river's right bank. A window in the castle opened, and a middle-aged woman leaned out to give the fleet a wave. The saturnine figure aboard the *Gabriel* turned and issued an order. The *Gabriel's* crew jumped to obey; flags floated up the mastheads, the guns were run out, and a salute echoed over the water in honor of the woman in the castle—Elizabeth, queen of England. A few moments later, a small boat left the shore and made for the *Gabriel*, bringing a royal messenger. The messenger addressed himself to the dark-haired man, saying that the queen was pleased with their actions and thanked them. She further requested that he, Martin Frobisher, as the commander of this daring expedition to find the Northwest Passage, present himself at court the next day to take his leave.

Queen Elizabeth's graciousness to Frobisher and his men signaled her approval of England's reentry into northwestern exploration. Although the reluctance of England's rulers to antagonize Spain had led them to discourage New World exploration in the years following Cabot's disappearance, Spain grew increasingly hostile nevertheless. In

Elizabeth I ruled England from 1558 to 1603. Her support of maritime exploration and other seafaring endeavors enabled her nation to supplant Spain as Europe's foremost naval power, a position it secured after its defeat of the great armada organized in 1588 by Philip II of Spain, whose offer of marriage Elizabeth had spurned in 1559.

Sebastian Cabot uses a pair of dividers to indicate the Arctic regions of the globe. Many of Cabot's contemporaries as well as later historians believed that his skills as a fabulist outshone his achievements as a mariner, but he was by all accounts a charming gentleman whose company and tales were always appreciated.

1544, King Charles I closed all of Spain's vast possessions to English ships, denying them entry to much of the European continent and all of America. English merchants, hard hit by this blow, began to look to the Mediterranean, Africa, and the waters north of Europe for new sources of income. In 1553 a group of them formed the Muscovy Company to sponsor trade exploration and named Sebastian Cabot as its chief. Voyages under Muscovy Company sponsorship managed over the succeeding decades to open English trade routes to Russia and to the Near East.

In 1558, Elizabeth Tudor, the 25-year-old daughter of King Henry VIII, succeeded to the throne of her embattled country. She proved to be a master of statecraft, wise, shrewd, and bold, and her courageous character and steadfast Protestantism in the face of the overwhelming might of Catholic Spain gave England a sense of national pride. Recognizing that England's national security depended on sea power, Good Queen Bess, as her affectionate subjects sometimes referred to her, encouraged English sailors to contest Portugal's supremacy in Africa and looked the other way as English pirates attacked Spanish shipping. In 1562, English ships began to smuggle African slaves into Spanish America. When Spanish warships attacked two English slave ships near Mexico in 1568, an undeclared war between the two countries broke out. With Elizabeth's approval, English privateers began to roam American waters.

At the same time in England, where a number of educated men had expounded on its existence and importance, interest in the Northwest Passage had reached new levels. The philosopher John Dee argued that northwest, northeast, and north polar routes must exist to balance the known passages around Africa and South America. In 1566, Sir Humphrey Gilbert, a Devonshire nobleman, wrote A *Discourse of a Discoverie for a New Passage to Cataia*, which glowingly described the wealth available to bold men who managed to penetrate the northwest route.

Ten years later, a group of London nobles and traders published the *Discourse* to promote an organization—later known as the Company of Cathay—formed for the purpose of northwest exploration. The group hired the spirited sea rover Martin Frobisher as the captain for its first expedition.

Burly, plainspoken, essentially unlettered, an individual, in his uncle John Frobisher's words, "of great spirit and bould courage and naturall hardnes of body," Frobisher had sailed as a lad of 14 on voyages to Africa, commanded privateers against Spain, fought with Gilbert against rebels in Ireland, and prowled the oceans as a pirate before agreeing to head the search. A longtime favorite of Queen Elizabeth's and a friend of Dee's and Gilbert's, he was known for his honesty, his courage, his leadership skills, and his violent temper. Frobisher threw himself into preparations for the voyage, supplying the ships with the latest navigational texts and a supply of the most advanced instruments (most of which he was unable to use). On June 7, 1576, his ships weighed anchor and headed down the Thames for Greenwich.

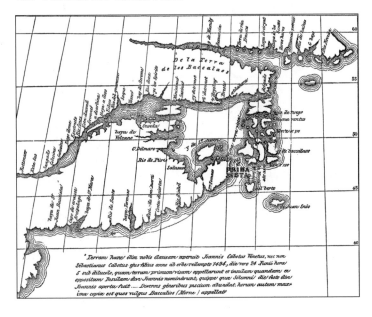

Gaspé Peninsula, the St. Lawrence River, and the Gulf of St. Lawrence, as seen in a detail from Sebastian Cabot's 1544 engraved map of the world. Cabot claimed to have sailed even farther north of this region on a 1508 voyage in search of the Northwest Passage, but many disbelieve his account.

Martin Frobisher believed that the discovery of the Northwest Passage was "the only thing left whereby a notable mind might be made famous and remarkable." It is doubtful that Frobisher's piratical past greatly troubled Queen Elizabeth, who tacitly encouraged English sailors to plunder Spanish shipping.

Frobisher planned to strike the American coast well to the north of Newfoundland. Accordingly, the three ships sailed northward up the east coast of Britain, arriving in the Shetland Islands on June 26. As the fleet headed westward across the Atlantic, a massive gale sank the pinnace, which took all hands with it to the bottom. Undaunted, Frobisher continued on. On July 11, a previously unknown coast appeared to the northwest, about 40 miles off. Christopher Hall, the *Gabriel*'s captain, wrote in his journal that mountains rose above the icebound coast "like pinnacles of steeples." Hall's recorded latitude of 61 degrees north reveals that the explorers were off the southeast coast of Greenland. Thick pack ice—what George Best, a member and chronicler of the expedition, called a "marvellous abundance of monstrous great islands of ice"—frustrated attempts to land and also thoroughly frightened the captain and crew of the *Michael*. As the astounded men of the *Gabriel* looked on, the *Michael* hoisted sail and made for home. When it reached London, its captain spread the story that the *Gabriel* had gone down with all hands.

The *Gabriel* was, however, far from finished. Frobisher held a conference with his 18 remaining officers and crew and decided to continue southward along the coast. Off Greenland's southern tip, a sudden squall knocked the ship flat on its side, sending water cascading down open hatchways. "With valiant courage," according to Best, Frobisher scuttled along the nearly vertical deck, cutting away lines and shrouds to relieve the wind pressure and ordering his panic-stricken crew to cut away the mizzenmast. The *Gabriel* righted itself but had to drift south until it could be pumped dry and a new mast could be rigged.

Turning to the northwest, the *Gabriel* sailed through open, frigid seas, occasionally encountering icebergs so massive that the explorers at first mistook them for land. On July 28, as the dawn sun cleared away a thick fog, the

Gabriel's lookout sighted a rocky, icebound promontory. Hall supposed it to be Labrador; in reality, the Englishmen had discovered Resolution Island, off the southeastern tip of Baffin Island, 900 miles northwest of Newfoundland. Ice again made a landing impossible, so Frobisher decided to follow the coast northward. At 4:00 A.M., lookouts spotted another headland to the northwest, separated from them, Best wrote, by "a great gutte, bay or passage, dividing as it were two mayne lands or continents asunder." Hopes that this was the passage soared. Icebergs, ever present at these latitudes, blocked the entrance to the strait; on August 1, one of them fell apart, making, as Captain Hall wrote, "a noyse as if a great cliffe had fallen into the sea." Finally, on August 11, the ice cleared, and the *Gabriel* sailed northwest into what Frobisher believed to be the strait.

Reveling in his apparent success, Frobisher decided that the strait must separate the continents of Asia and America. With exuberant self-confidence he named his passage Frobisher's Straits. Throughout the month of August, the *Gabriel* continued along the northern coast of the passage, occasionally stopping to explore islands. At some point, Frobisher ordered his men to pick up anything interesting ashore as a sign of English possession. One of the men came back with a chunk of black rock that seemed to contain minerals. Frobisher thought it unimportant but kept it as evidence of his discovery.

On August 18, the explorers dropped anchor off an island some 150 miles from the entrance to the passage. The next day, Frobisher, Hall, and eight men rowed ashore to search for inhabitants. From the top of a hill Hall spotted floating objects approaching that he at first took to be porpoises, but the indistinct figures soon resolved themselves into fur-clad natives in kayaks. Hall recorded in his journal that "they bee like to Tartars, with long blacke haire, broad faces, and flatte noses, and tawnie in

(continued on page 54)

Down to the Sea in Ships

He is an *Otter*, an *Amphibian* that lives both on Land and Water . . . his familiarity with death and danger, hath armed him with a kind of dissolute security against any encounter. The sea cannot roar more abroad, than he within, fire him but with liquor. . . . In a Tempest you shall hear him pray, but so amethodically, as it argues that he is seldom versed in that practice. . . . He makes small or no choice of his pallet; he can sleep as well on a Sack of Pumice as a pillow of down. He was never much acquainted with civility; the Sea has taught him other Rhetoric. He is most constant to his shirt, and other his seldom washed linen. He has been so long acquainted with the surges of the Sea, as too long a calm distempers him. He cannot speak low, the Sea talks so loud. . . . He can spin up a rope like a Spider, and down again like lightning. . . . Death he has seen in so many shapes, as it cannot amaze him.

Thus did Richard Braithwaite portray "A Sailor" in his 1631 book, *Whimsies, or New Cast of Characters.* But if the typical seafaring man that Braithwaite described seems somewhat unfit for polite society, that is perhaps understandable given the shipboard conditions under which he labored. Wages were paltry: 5 shillings a day for a seaman in the Royal Navy during the time of Henry VII, 10 shillings a day for the men of Frobisher's second voyage. Meals were prepared over a fire, either inside a small hooded shelter, called a cookbox, on deck, or more likely, on transatlantic voyages, inside an enclosed room beneath a forward deck. Repasts were necessarily limited in variety. On Frobisher's second voyage, for example, his men were allotted each day a quarter pound of butter, a half pound of cheese, and a pound of biscuit—the dreaded hardtack—made of flour and water. Some honey was available for sweetening, and several casks of vinegar were also stored on board. On certain specified "flesh days," each sailor would be given a pound of salt beef or pork, which was packed in brine to keep it from spoiling. A single dried codfish served four sailors on religious feast days; when the fish ran out, rice and oatmeal took its place. English sailors washed down this fare with beer (Frobisher's men were apportioned a gallon a day), French and Spanish seafarers with wine. Few sea dogs would touch water until the casks of alcoholic beverages were exhausted.

The colorfulness of marine garb was in sharp contrast to the drabness of the shipboard diet, but here too seafaring men suffered from a want of variety. Most sailors wore a hooded gown of coarse cloth, loose trousers, and long woolen stockings. Shoes were saved for onshore visits; because leather skids on wet wood, mariners performed most of their duties barefoot. Bright blues and reds were the preferred colors for gowns and "trews," but because sailors had to provide their own clothing, they rarely had spare garments to change into. On Frobisher's well-equipped second voyage, his men were given up to six extra sets of clothing, but such sartorial concern was rare. Even on northern voyages, no special cold-weather gear was provided. Sailors wore their clothes until they rotted or fell off; in the early 17th century, a correspondent to the Admiralty cited the "nasty beastliness to which the men are subject by the continual wearing of one set of clothes."

There was an even greater source of "beastliness" on board: the hold. Bilge pumps were kept constantly busy freeing the hold not only of seawater leakage but of vomit, urine, excrement, and food remains. Small wonder that maritime chronicles constantly mention the "foul stinks" and "pestilential funks" emanating from below, and that both Frobisher and Sebastian Cabot were moved to emphasize to their men the benefits of shipboard cleanliness. Lack of sanitation bred vermin, and seagoing vessels were notorious for the number, size, and ferocity of their cockroaches and rats. Most ships carried at least two cats to deal with rodent passengers.

At night, the weary mariner eager for a dreamy escape from this mean existence—if only for the four hours until the change of watch—flopped down on deck wherever he could find a spot. Cabins and bunks were reserved for the captain and maybe a couple of officers. Is it any surprise that Braithwaite describes his "amphibian" as "never much acquainted with civility"?

A woodcut of a typical 16th-century sailing vessel.

(continued from page 51)

color, wearing Seale skinnes." The Eskimo traded furs for English iron tools and on one occasion tested the awareness of the English by trying to steal the *Gabriel's* boat. On August 20, Frobisher invited one of the natives aboard ship. After a brief visit, he sent five men with the ship's boat to take the Eskimo back, with explicit instructions to set him on a rock far away from the main crowd of natives. The sailors, eager to trade, disobeyed, and landed in the Eskimo's midst. The natives jumped the sailors and carried them, struggling, out of sight.

Frobisher evidently did not want to risk any more men in a pursuit. The next day he sailed the *Gabriel* close to shore and ordered a gun fired and a trumpet sounded. After getting no response from the missing men, he moved away to anchor in safety. One day later he returned, in the *Gabriel*, to the scene of the kidnapping. When lookouts spotted kayaks approaching, Frobisher ordered the ship cleared for action. The crew jumped to stretch canvas screens across the *Gabriel's* low sides and to load the ship's guns. The Eskimo backed off, although Frobisher did succeed in luring one courageous—or foolhardy—fellow alongside the *Gabriel*, whereupon the husky mariner hauled him on board and took him captive. Now down to 13 exhausted men, Frobisher decided not to risk continuing his voyage. On August 26, the *Gabriel* weighed anchor and headed southeast, reaching open sea by evening of the next day. On October 2, after a smooth crossing, the *Gabriel* dropped anchor in the Thames.

When news spread that Frobisher had discovered a northwest passage to China, he received a joyous welcome. Had Frobisher sailed a mere 25 miles northwest of his final anchorage, however, he would have learned that the straits end, forming what is today called Frobisher Bay. But no one in London knew this, of course, and Frobisher became the hero of the hour. Excitement increased when someone noticed goldlike flakes in Frobisher's piece of black rock. When an Italian mineralogist declared the rock to be gold ore, a second expedition was organized with great haste. Frobisher's merchant supporters provided him again with two ships—the *Gabriel* and the *Michael*, presumably captained and manned this time by a more steadfast complement of seamen—and Queen Elizabeth paid for another, the 200-ton *Aid*. This time out, Frobisher's mission was to mine more ore; further exploration of the strait was to take place only if he had the time. Accordingly, his crew of more than 150 men included miners as well as sailors. About 35 soldiers were also on board, as was a painter, John White, who would be the first European to visually portray the Eskimo. (White would go on to attain even greater fame for his paintings and drawings of the Jamestown colony in Virginia.) Six convicted criminals rounded out the crew; they were put ashore on Greenland to "civilize" the natives.

The trio of ships departed England on May 30, 1577. After a summer spent mining a small island in Frobisher Bay, skirmishing occasionally with the Eskimo, and searching fruitlessly for the 5 missing sailors, Frobisher

A German artist, Lucas de Heere, created this woodcut of an Eskimo man hunting birds with a spear from a kayak, after witnessing a similar exhibition performed in the harbor at Bristol by an Eskimo captured by Frobisher on his second voyage. The Eskimo woman and child in the illustration had also been taken by Frobisher. The background is the artist's imaginative re-creation of the landscape of Frobisher Bay. De Heere has given the male Eskimo a bushy beard, of the type then favored by European men, but Eskimos rarely, if ever, grow full facial hair.

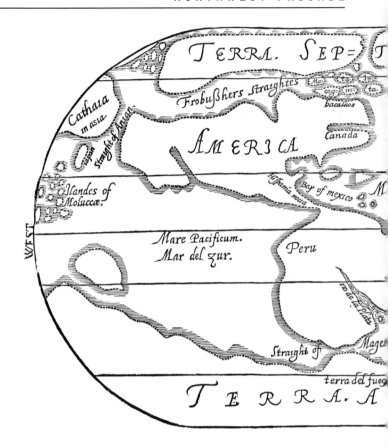

George Best, who sailed with Frobisher on all three voyages and penned an account of the expeditions, published this map in 1578. It illustrates the prevailing European conception of the Northwest Passage as a clear strait above North America leading directly to China (Cathaia on this map).

returned with 200 tons of the black rock in the holds of his ships. Two reputable German mineralogists declared the ore to contain considerable profits in gold, so in 1578 yet another expedition was dispatched. Half the cost of this ambitious venture was underwritten by Elizabeth, the other half by the Company of Cathay; Frobisher sailed this time at the head of a fleet of 15 ships. Confused by a snowstorm, Frobisher sailed too far south and inadvertently entered what is known today as Hudson Bay. There, the crew observed a furious current coming from the west that was occasionally strong enough to spin a ship completely around. After recognizing his mistake, Frobisher continued on, torn between his obligations to his backers, by whom he had been charged to establish a permanent mining operation, and his desire to explore. Duty ulti-

mately won out, and Frobisher ordered his fleet to turn about and leave what he had named the "Mistaken Straits."

Misconceptions continued to bedevil the stalwart mariner. For 5 years after his return to England in September 1578, the Company of Cathay sought to extract gold from the 1,350 tons of ore Frobisher had brought back, but in 1583 honest assayers finally revealed the rock to be worthless. The company went bankrupt, Frobisher was accused of intentionally defrauding the company's stockholders, and the scandal derailed his career. He returned to privateering and later redeemed himself through his service in defeating the Spanish Armada, as the tremendous naval flotilla sent by Philip II against England in 1588 was known. Frobisher's heroism on that occasion won him a knighthood; he died in 1594 leading an assault against a Spanish fortress.

That Frobisher's gold had proven to be dross did not discourage the masterminds of the Company of Cathay. In 1585, Adrian Gilbert (Sir Humphrey's brother), John Dee, and others persuaded the powerful London merchant William Sanderson to support a new expedition. Sanderson promptly recommended, in the words of his assistant John Janes, "one M. John Davis, a man very well grounded in the principles of the Arte of Navigation, for Captaine and chiefe Pilot of this exployt." The 36-year-old Davis was living in retirement on his country farm after a successful career as a privateer, but the associates

Sir Humphrey Gilbert, an influential supporter of Frobisher and John Davis, received his knighthood in 1570 for dispossessing Irish Catholics of their land, but it was a treatise he penned seven years later, How Her Majesty may annoy the King of Spain, *that truly won him Queen Elizabeth's admiration. In 1583, she provided him with the ships, men, and supplies that enabled him to found England's first colony in the New World, at St. John's, Newfoundland.*

convinced him to take up command of the new expedition. Two small barks were fitted out for the voyage in the southwestern port of Dartmouth: the *Sunneshine*, 50 tons, and the *Mooneshine*, 35 tons, manned with a combined crew of 42 men.

The two ships sailed to the northwest from Dartmouth on June 7, 1585. Six weeks later, on July 19, the vessels entered a massive fog bank so thick that the crew of the *Sunneshine* lost sight of its companion completely. The air was filled with a great roaring sound, like waves crashing on the beach. When Davis and Janes went out in the *Sunneshine*'s boat to investigate, they found that huge icebergs crashing together were creating the terrifying concussions. When the fog lifted the next day, the mariners were presented with a view of the "most deformed, rockie, and mountainous land that ever we saw." A snow-covered mountain towered in the background; miles of ice blocked the coast as far as the eye could see. What the awestruck sailors were gazing upon was the east coast of Greenland; Davis named it the "Land of Desolation." After increasing rations all around to improve his shaken crew's flagging morale, Davis took his ships around Greenland's tip, then headed north. On July 29, a lookout spotted land bearing northeast. As the ships neared the coast, the crew was able to distinguish numerous islands and inlets; the numerous rocky cliffs visible "were all of such oare as M. Frobisher brought." Davis named his discovery Gilbert Sound, after Sir Humphrey Gilbert, who had been lost at sea 2 years earlier; his records reveal it to be the entrance to Godthåb Harbor, located some 400 miles north-northwest of Greenland's tip. When Davis and some of his men, in a ship's boat, landed on one of the islands, a group of Eskimo rowed up to investigate. Davis hurriedly sent to the *Mooneshine* for the ship's four musicians, who piped a merry tune while the English sailors danced for the natives' benefit. The Englishmen presented the Eskimo with small gifts and continued "playing with our musicke, and making signs of joy, and dauncing" until nightfall. The next day the Eskimo returned, convinced that the English were friends, and brisk trading ensued.

On the first day of August, Davis took his ships to the northwest, across a stretch of ocean now known as the Davis Strait. A week later the explorers came in sight of a bare, mountainous land where moderate temperatures had kept the coast completely clear of ice. Davis named a mountain for Sir Walter Raleigh, poet, soldier, explorer, Sir Humphrey Gilbert's half brother, and Elizabeth's favorite courtier; and a cape for Sir Francis Walsingham, the queen's secretary and a longtime proponent of northwest exploration. These names have endured; Cape Walsingham and Mount Raleigh are located on the west coast of Baffin Island, 150 miles northeast of Frobisher Bay. Near Mount Raleigh, Davis's men killed four "white bears of a monstrous bignesse." Davis then ordered the ships southward.

On August 11, as the ships floated through a deep fog, the coast seemed to disappear, leaving only open water to the west. When the fog broke, the explorers found themselves in a broad sound, in some places as wide as 50 miles across, that appeared to stretch limitlessly ahead to the northwest. Davis named it Cumberland Sound in honor of a noble supporter, the earl of Cumberland. The ships sailed along its northern coast, the crew searching with mounting elation for signs that it had found a passage between oceans, Davis noting that the water remained the same dark color as open sea. A few days into the strait, lookouts spotted a school of whales coming from the west. A strong current flowed west to east, and the water became deeper and deeper, until at last, even using a 330-fathom lead, or length of rope (a fathom equals 6 feet), the crew was unable to find bottom. Like others before him, Davis interpreted these signs to mean that his quest for the Northwest Passage had succeeded. On August 20, while the ships were some 180 miles from the entrance to the strait, the wind shifted to the northwest, halting their progress. Davis decided that he had come far enough and ordered his ships about. After exploring the southern coast on the way out, the fleet reached the strait's entrance on August 24 and Dartmouth on September 30.

Upon his return, Davis informed Walsingham of his certainty of the existence and location of the long-elusive passage. "The northwest passage is a matter nothing doubtful, but at anytime to be passed," Davis wrote, "the sea navigable, voyd of yce, the ayre tolerable, and the waters very depe." Presented with such assurance, Davis's backers renewed their support and underwrote a second expedition. In addition to the *Mooneshine* and the *Sunneshine*, Davis received the 120-ton *Mermayd* and the little 10-ton pinnace *Northe Starre*. On May 11, 1586, the fleet left Ireland behind them and set course northwest.

Several weeks out, Davis divided his fleet, sending the *Sunneshine* and the *Northe Starre* north along the eastern coast of Greenland to investigate John Dee's theory of an arctic passage. It was Dee's contention that because, as was known, the sun shone for months at a time in the extreme northern latitudes, it would melt the ice caps that had barred the way of earlier expeditions, leaving a free passage to the East. But the crews of the *Sunneshine* and the *North Starre* lost heart well before reaching the Arctic Circle and turned around and headed back to England, although the tiny *North Starre* was lost somewhere en route and never made it home. Meanwhile, on June 29, the remaining ships dropped anchor in Gilbert Sound, where a second pinnace, which had been stowed in the *Mermayd*'s hold, was assembled and rigged. On July 17, the augmented fleet set off to the north.

The sailors faced a colder summer than they had the year before. Shortly after leaving Gilbert Sound, the ships fell in with an iceberg so huge that, like Frobisher's men, Davis's crew first mistook it for land. The three ships

The Welsh wizard John Dee was tried in England's notorious Star Chamber for practicing sorcery against Queen Mary I, but he enjoyed the favor of her sister and successor, Elizabeth. An alchemist, mathematician, and astrologer, Dee was an enthusiastic advocate of maritime exploration and was one of the founders of the Company of Cathay, but he left England in 1585 after a spirit summoned at a séance convinced him that his colleagues were in league against him.

This late-16th-century woodcut shows mariners in a ship's boat rowing mightily in an attempt to free their larger vessel from the arctic ice, while ashore some other members of the crew hunt a polar bear. Davis's failures in locating the Northwest Passage did not lessen his certainty of its existence, and English mariners continued the search despite the hardships of arctic exploration.

coasted the frosty glacial remnant for two weeks, until the ships' masts, sails, and rigging were sheathed in ice. Suffering bitterly from the cold, the sailors asked Davis to turn about. After failing to sway them, Davis agreed to send those that wanted to leave back to England in the *Mermayd*.

His remaining ships made landfall on Baffin Island at almost the same place they had the year before. Davis then ordered a southward course, similar to the previous year's, but for some reason, perhaps bad weather, he did not recognize Cumberland Sound. On August 19, the two remaining ships reached the entrance to Frobisher Bay, where Davis climbed to a high hill on Resolution Island and looked around but was still unable to recognize his location. (Davis was hampered, at this point, by his reliance on Frobisher's often spectacularly misguided charts, which were in turn based on a notoriously wrongheaded, if not outrightly fraudulent, conception of northern geography known as the Zeno map.) Davis failed to note the entrance to what would become known as Hudson Strait, perhaps because ice blocked it from view. With increasing frustration, he ordered the search continued southward, without success. The *Mooneshine* and the pinnace continued down the Labrador coast until the beginning of September, exploring inlets that looked promising. Finally, after losing part of a shore party in a skirmish with "the brutish people of this country," as Davis described the indigenous inhabitants, and barely surviving a violent storm, Davis took his fleet home. The two ships arrived in England in early October 1586.

Despite his failure, Davis remained optimistic. He wrote to William Sanderson, "I am assured [the passage] must be in one of foure places, or els not at all" and vowed to sell his family estate, if need be, "to see an end of these businesses." Such confidence was enough for his financial backers, who agreed to fund a third voyage. Davis sailed from Dartmouth on May 19, 1587, with the *Sunneshine*, a new ship named the *Elizabeth*, and a pinnace of dubious seaworthiness, the *Ellen*. On June 12 the crew of the *Sunneshine* threatened to mutiny; having heard of the easy fishing near Newfoundland, they preferred a quick profit to the hazards of exploration. Four days later the fleet dropped anchor in Gilbert Sound, where the men of the crew again grew restless. In order to prevent outright rebellion, Davis released the *Sunneshine* and the *Elizabeth*, setting a rendezvous on the Labrador coast for August.

On June 21, Davis and John Janes set off with a few men in the undersized *Ellen*, sailing northward up the Greenland coast. The pinnace crossed the Arctic Circle and on June 24 stopped to trade with a few hardy Eskimo who paddled their kayaks 30 miles out to sea to bargain for iron tools. On June 30, Davis reached a harbor 600 miles north of Gilbert Sound. In these latitudes, reported Janes, the sun still lay five degrees above the horizon at midnight. High, craggy cliffs overlooked a curving harbor where a snow-covered peak towered in the background. Davis named this harbor "Sanderson's Hope"; it is now the site of the Greenland town of Upernavik.

Although open water beckoned to the north, a shift in the wind forced Davis to set his course to the west. Initially, the *Ellen* met only open ocean, but on July 2 it found its way blocked by the huge mass of pack ice that yearly breaks away from the polar ice cap and streams down the center of Davis Strait. Davis sailed south trying to get around the icy barrier and succeeded in rounding the ice pack's southern tip on July 16. Two days later, Davis recognized Mount Raleigh, and by midnight on July 19 the *Ellen* lay off the entrance to Cumberland Sound. The next morning the tiny ship pushed northwest; in the next 3 days it covered 160 miles, discovering, in the process, the landlocked end of Cumberland Sound. No doubt weary and sick with disappointment, Davis returned to the open sea and headed south for the planned rendezvous with the remainder of his fleet.

On July 31, after passing Frobisher Bay, the mariners crossed "a very great gulfe, the water whirling and roaring as it were the meeting of tydes." This was the same current pouring out of Hudson Strait that Frobisher's men had noticed in 1578, but Davis did not hazard a closer reconnaissance, either because of thick ice or from the desire not to miss the reunion with the *Sunneshine* and the *Elizabeth*. On August 15, having reached Belle Isle Strait without a sign of the other ships, Davis decided to brave the Atlantic alone; the trusty *Ellen* rewarded his confidence by bringing the sailors safely into Dartmouth Harbor a month later. The *Sunneshine* and the *Elizabeth* had long since arrived, their holds stuffed full of cod.

Despite this final setback, Davis remained convinced of the Northwest Passage's existence, although he now decided that it must lie in the presumably open waters north of Sanderson's Hope. "I have bene in 73 degrees, finding the sea all open and 40 leagues between land and land," he wrote to Sanderson. "The passage is most probable, the execution easie." But his backers had run out of money and interest, and Davis never returned to northern waters. None the richer in titles or wealth as a result of his search for the Northwest Passage, he nevertheless continued to devote himself to the sea and exploration. In the 18 years left him before his death in 1605 at the hands of Japanese pirates off Singapore, he commanded a vessel in England's victory over the Spanish Armada; sailed with Sir Walter Raleigh on several voyages of exploration; discovered the Falkland Islands, which lie some 300 miles east of the Strait of Magellan, at the southern tip of Argentina, and remain one of the last vestiges of the British Empire; wrote several treatises on navigation (Davis's latitude readings from his northern voyages, aided by his use of the backstaff and the Davis quadrant—instruments of his own invention that were used for centuries after his death—were remarkably accurate); and made three voyages to the East

Indies. His legacy remains the names he gave to features of the Baffin Island and Labrador coasts and the honor of having his name given to the strait between Greenland and North America, as well as the notion that his adventures helped instill in his countrymen—the conviction, as Davis himself put it, that as concerns seamanship, the English "are not to be matched by any nation of the earth." Through the centuries to come, this pride in its nautical prowess would sustain the island nation in its ongoing quest for the maddeningly elusive Northwest Passage.

In 1588, King Philip II of Spain assembled a great fleet of 130 ships, carrying 27,000 men, that was to spearhead an invasion of England designed to restore that country to Catholicism. The Spanish Armada was believed to be invincible, but the English fleet, including ships commanded by Frobisher and Davis, utilized its superior maneuverability and firepower to rout the flotilla.

Mutiny in Hudson Bay

In May 1609, the small two-masted Dutch trading ship *Half Moon* lay idle in the ice-filled Barents Sea, northeast of Finland. Of about 80 tons burden, broad and flat bottomed, the *Half Moon* was built to navigate shallow coastal waters, not to force its way through pack ice. Its English commander, 40-year-old Henry Hudson, a mariner of obscure antecedents and background who may have sailed with Davis, faced a difficult situation. He had long since lost hope of reaching China by discovering a northeast passage to the north of Russia, as his sponsors in the Netherlands had charged him with doing. Among his 20-man crew—some Dutch, some English—unrest mounted as national rivalry and the futility of the voyage stretched cold and tired nerves to their limits. Hudson, a brilliant navigator but sometimes ineffectual leader, offered his crew a choice. Their employers, the Dutch East India Company, wanted to find a quick passage to the Far East and did not care much where they found it. Two northwestern possibilities beckoned: a passage reported by Hudson's friend Captain John Smith to be located near his Virginia Colony, and Captain Davis's "very great gulfe" south of Frobisher Bay.

Hudson had considered the possible existence of a northwest passage during two previous arctic voyages. In 1607 and 1608, the Muscovy Company had sent him north, first to make another attempt on John Dee's polar

Henry Hudson (left) was apparently an able navigator but less adept as a leader of men, although some historians believe he has been unjustly maligned. They point out that Abacuck Prickett's portrayal of Hudson's last voyage, which is the only surviving eyewitness account, may have been influenced by Prickett's interest in portraying himself and his shipmates in a favorable light.

route, then to try the northeastern passage. When both failed, the company lost interest, but Hudson did not remain unemployed for long. In early 1609, the Dutch, who had replaced Spain as England's great trade rival after the defeat of the Spanish Armada, invited him to give an account of his explorations to the directors of the Dutch East India Company. After some consideration, the company fitted out the *Half Moon* and gave Hudson the command with orders to search either east or west for a passage.

After having traveled no farther to the east than he had the year before, Hudson let his rebellious crew determine the next step. The sailors, eager to trade ice for a milder climate, chose the southern route. On July 18, the *Half Moon* reached the forested coast of Maine, where a damaged foremast forced Hudson to anchor for repairs. While carpenters replaced the mast, some of the crew went ashore to trade with the natives, but the unruly men soon began to mistreat and steal from the Indians, forcing Hudson to sail on July 26 to avoid attack. For two and a half weeks the *Half Moon* sailed south, mostly out of sight of land. On August 12, lookouts sighted Chesapeake Bay, the entrance to the Virginia Colony. Perhaps because his vessel flew a Dutch flag, Hudson decided against sailing up to Jamestown to consult with Captain Smith, opting instead to leave the bay behind and look for his passage to the north.

For the rest of August, the *Half Moon* sailed the mid-Atlantic coast, pausing briefly in Delaware Bay. On September 3, Hudson's men came upon the same view that had impressed Verrazano 85 years before: a broad inlet leading north, flanked by two wooded highlands. Hudson's mate, Robert Juet, wrote that "the lands were pleasant with grass and flowers and goodly trees . . . very sweet smells came from them." As the *Half Moon* dropped anchor in the Narrows, throngs of natives dressed in deerskins paddled out, eager to trade tobacco for knives and beads. Not all was peaceful, however; a few days later, warriors killed an English sailor, and Hudson ordered two hostages taken in reprisal.

On September 12, the *Half Moon*'s crew hoisted sail and entered the great river at the north end of the Upper Bay. Hudson paused briefly to land on the large island called by the natives Manna-hata. In his journal, Hudson described Manhattan Island as "as pleasant a land as one can tread upon, very abundant in all kinds of timber suitable for shipbuilding." As the little ship proceeded, Juet noted that "the river is a mile broad. There is very high land on both sides. The river is full of fish." On September 14, the *Half Moon* passed between two points overlooking the river; the promontory on the left bank is possibly the site—West Point—chosen by George Washington in the 18th century for a fort and later a military academy. All along the explorers' route, friendly natives rowed out to trade food for trinkets or to invite the Europeans ashore.

As the late summer days passed and the *Half Moon* continued northward, the country to the west of the river grew mountainous. On the morning of September 17, the ship passed a group of islands in midstream, and its crew began to notice shallow water. A couple of days later, Hudson ordered the *Half Moon* anchored near the site of modern-day Albany, New York. On September 20, Hudson sent five men upriver in the ship's boat; they returned and reported that the river dwindled to a depth of two fathoms after five miles. Two days later, Hudson sent the boat out again. This time, the sailors reported the river unnavigable. The next day, convinced that the river was not the strait, Hudson ordered his men to make sail for open sea.

The return trip passed as before, except for a running battle with Indian braves that lasted from the area of Stony Point to the northern tip of Manhattan. On October 4, the *Half Moon* left New York Bay and entered the Atlantic. Once more, Hudson convened a council of his officers to decide the next move. A Dutch mate advised wintering

A musketeer in the Barents expedition fires at a polar bear but is too late to save his companion from the jaws of the arctic predator. Willem Barents was a Dutch explorer who in the 1590s attempted twice to reach the East via the so-called Northeast Passage—over the top of Europe and Russia. Like Barents, Hudson also attempted the Northeast Passage, and both men died at sea.

Indians watch from shore as the Half Moon *sails up the great river in New York State that bears Hudson's name. Like so many explorers, Hudson profited not at all from his discoveries.*

in Newfoundland and searching for a passage in the Davis Strait the following spring, but with provisions running low and a surly, mutinous crew to contend with, Hudson was reluctant to risk an extension of his voyage. He decided instead to make for England, and on November 7 the *Half Moon* docked in Dartmouth, from where Hudson sent news of his findings to the Amsterdam entrepreneurs who had commissioned his venture.

Word of a new river route to the rich interior of the North American continent was equally welcome to England's merchants (especially the directors of the British East India Company, formed in 1600 for the purpose of sponsoring trading expeditions to the Far East), its king, James I, and his ministers. England and the newly independent Netherlands had embarked on a fierce maritime rivalry, centered on exploiting the American and Indies trade previously dominated by the Spanish and the Portuguese. As had been true for centuries, the nation that found a new route to the East would benefit greatly, and both England and the Netherlands were eager to profit from such ancillary advantages of the search for the Northwest Passage as claims to new regions of North America. Accordingly, James I ordered the commander and crew of the *Half Moon* held and the ship and its records seized, and Hudson was persuaded that his next voyage, underwritten by some prominent London men of business and encouraged by the Prince of Wales, should be conducted for his native land. The 55-ton *Discoverie* was fitted out in London for Hudson, who was, according to the 17th-century chronicler Samuel Purchas, "to try if through any of those inlets which Davis saw but durst not enter any passage might be found to the . . . South Sea."

The *Discoverie* set sail on April 17, 1610. The ill-tempered and often drunken Juet again accompanied Hudson as mate; the friction between these two was so considerable that one must wonder, as historians have done, why they continued to agree to keep close company with one another on a strenuous ocean voyage. Some of Hudson's other choices for the crew were equally ill advised. A former haberdasher with the unlikely name of Abacuck Prickett, whose account of the ill-starred voyage forms the basis for much of what is known about Hudson's fate, proved fairly reliable, but William Wilson was an inveterate sower of dissent, and Henry Greene, whom Hudson made a special stop for but insisted on omitting from the official ship's roster, had to that point, according to Prickett, embraced a "lewd life" that had cost him "the good will of all his friends." Shipboard scuttlebutt had it that Hudson and Greene were lovers.

The explorers sighted Davis's "Land of Desolation" in early June and rounded Greenland's tip on June 15. Over the next few days, the tiny bark sailed northwest through seas full of icebergs, some large enough, according to Purchas, "whereon they might runne and play." On June 24 the men sighted the rugged coast south of Frobisher Bay. The next morning, in a thick fog, the rising tide swept the *Discoverie* westward into the broad inlet that now bears Hudson's name. As the fog cleared and the *Discoverie*'s crew took soundings, the depth and breadth of the strait led Hudson to dare to hope that he had found the Northwest Passage. For 500 miles the ship sailed west among icebergs and small islands, its crew sighting land on both sides of the strait from time to time. Finally, after more than a month, the *Discoverie* rounded a headland to the south and entered open water that appeared to stretch limitlessly to the south and west. An ecstatic Hudson named it the "bay of God's great mercies"; it is better known as Hudson Bay.

Throughout August and September, Hudson followed the coast southward, but October brought trouble. Shallow soundings revealed to Hudson that he had sailed the *Discoverie* into a dead end. This cul-de-sac, 600 miles south of the Hudson Strait, is now called James Bay. Frittering away the remaining days before the onset of winter, Hudson spent weeks sailing back and forth across the bay trying to find a passage leading west, without success. His indecision cost him the always questionable loyalty of Juet, who openly threatened to seize the ship and head home. A court-martial was held on board, and Juet was relieved of his position. Finally, at the beginning of November, Hudson made the fateful decision to spend the winter anchored in a small cove, despite the ship's almost complete lack of provisions and his crew's unpreparedness for a winter at sea.

On November 10, ice surrounded the *Discoverie*, freezing it in place. Hudson initially refused to allow his men to build a shelter ashore; by the time he changed his mind, the shore was covered with snow and ice and the ship's carpenter refused to leave the *Discoverie*. Increasingly unpredictable, Hudson battered the unfortunate woodworker around the head and threatened to string him up. Further dissension was aroused by Hudson's arbitrary award to Greene, his favorite, of an overcoat, highly coveted under the circumstances, that had belonged to a deceased sailor. (Customary procedure called for the dead sailor's belongings to be auctioned off among all the crew.) Then, in a fit of jealousy over Greene's behavior, Hudson took the coat from him and gave it to Robert Bylot, the steady, even-keeled navigator.

As the long winter progressed, food ran desperately low. The Englishmen managed to survive by catching a few birds and fish, but they suffered—just like Cartier's group, who had found themselves in similar circumstances—from scurvy. Tempers flared among the *Discoverie*'s company. Hudson grew increasingly autocratic, causing widespread resentment by insisting on searching the sea chests of each member of his crew for hoarded food. The crew in turn suspected their commander of secreting rations away for his favorites.

In the late spring of 1611, when the ice surrounding the ship finally began to break, the starving men rejoiced

(continued on page 81)

The Hid Secret of Nature

Sebastian Cabot's interest in exploration was not limited to the search for the Northwest Passage; as head of the Muscovy Company, he also sponsored missions to the Northeast Passage.

The hid secret of nature" is how Sebastian Cabot characterized the Northwest Passage, and indeed few objects of exploratory quests succeeded in so long frustrating their seekers. More than three centuries elapsed between John Cabot's first voyage west in search of a passage to Asia and the eventual completion of the search by English explorers in the mid-19th century. By contrast, the Portuguese found their passage to the Indies within 80 years of the first voyages dispatched for that purpose by Prince Henry the Navigator, and Ferdinand Magellan discovered his strait through the Americas the first time he set out to look for it. By the time of the ill-starred Franklin expedition of 1845, there seemed to be no practical reason for continuing the search: The frigid regions in question had long since been claimed by England, and the passage, if it existed, would have no practical commercial value. But man's desire to confront the unknown overrode such considerations, and the Northwest Passage continued to exert an irresistible allure.

John Cabot accepts the well wishes of merchants
and clergymen on the quay at Bristol before departing
on his 1497 voyage.

There are apparently no existing
portraits of Giovanni da Verrazano
done from life; this likeness was painted
by Orazio Fidani in the early 17th
century. Verrazano died in 1528,
82 years before Fidani was born.

Indians, presumably Huron, watch as Jacques Cartier and his men make their way up the St. Lawrence River, which, Cartier wrote, "flows between high mountains of bare rock, which nevertheless support a vast quantity of trees

The aurora borealis illuminates the awesome isolation of an arctic ship trapped for the long winter in the ice, as depicted in a 19th-century painting by Frederic Church. It was not uncommon for northern explorers to spend months and even years stranded aboard their vessels under such conditions.

This portrait of Cartier was commissioned by his hometown of Saint-Malo in the 19th century. Here, Cartier presents a rather stern and gloomy visage, but church records in Saint-Malo record the explorer as a frequent and enthusiastic participant in baptismal and marital celebrations. In 1550, Cartier entertained Sebastian Cabot at his home, and the two aging mariners regaled each other with tall tales of their past exploits.

In this 1881 painting by John Collier, a frightened and
inappropriately clad John Hudson looks to his father, Henry, for
consolation as the small boat in which they have been marooned
drifts between massive icebergs. Like many of those who lost
their lives in the search for the Northwest Passage, Henry
Hudson owed his tragic fate in large part to his own folly.

(continued from page 72)

to see an enormous school of fish surround the *Discoverie*. Hudson, however, could not wait to get under way. In June, before stores could be completely replenished, he ordered sails set for England. At the same time, he ordered Bylot removed as first mate and replaced with Philip Staffe, the carpenter, and confiscated all the navigational instruments on board. These actions led the crew to fear for their safety, for all, including Hudson, had come to rely on Bylot's navigational skills, and Staffe could neither read nor write. Hudson attempted to placate his crew by releasing all the remaining stores of bread (about a pound per man) and cheese (three and a half pounds per man), but this proved disastrous: Predictably, the men, near starvation from their long winter on extremely shortened rations, bolted down the food and grew extremely angry upon discovering that there was none left. Continued rumors that Hudson was hoarding supplies, as well as Staffe's remark that the commander had acted justly in allocating rations unequally, for some men were more valuable than others, added fuel to the flames of rebellion.

On the night of June 22, 1611, angry sailors, led by the disgruntled Juet, seized Hudson as he slept in his cabin. The mutineers set him, his teenage son John, and

This detail from a 17th-century French map shows the Atlantic seaboard regions of Canada. Cartier's voyages in search of the Northwest Passage provided one basis for France's claims in the St. Lawrence River valley, while Hudson's voyages helped give England a foothold to the north and west.

This copper engraving from 1596 shows a ship of the Barents expedition trapped in the polar ice. For Hudson's crew, the long months spent in James Bay while the Discoverie *was held fast by the winter ice ended whatever respect they still possessed for their commander.*

a few loyal men, including the beleaguered carpenter, adrift in the *Discoverie's* boat and left them to fend for themselves on the icy waters. Ailing from scurvy, Prickett argued against the scheme, only to be told by Greene that "he would rather be hanged at home than starved abroad." Subsequent investigation of Hudson's quarters turned up substantial quantities of biscuit, grain, and beer.

The remaining crew struggled homeward. Eskimo killed several ringleaders of the mutiny, including Wilson and Greene, near the western entrance to Hudson Strait, prompting Purchas to write, "Everywhere can Divine Justice find executioners." Juet died of starvation before the *Discoverie* reached England, but Bylot took command and

brought the tiny ship home virtually single-handed, for the other seven survivors were by then too weak to help.

News of the cruel end of the Hudson expedition aroused both excitement and revulsion. Hope ran high that the great bay Hudson had discovered was indeed the passage, and the evident suffering of the surviving mutineers, the belief that Hudson might still be alive, the earlier death of the ringleaders, and the ample evidence of Hudson's erratic behavior contributed to the comparatively lenient treatment received by the survivors. (Only four were tried, some seven years after their return; none was convicted.) New voyages to the northwest were planned, with the Prince of Wales providing departing captains with explicit instructions designed to prevent repeats of the unfortunate Hudson episode. Daily prayers were required on ship, the sabbath was to be honored, and drunkenness, profanity, dissension, and sodomy were to be dealt with harshly.

Hudson's merchant backers remained enthusiastic about northwest exploration and consolidated into the Northwest Passage Company in order to sponsor new voyages. Between 1612 and 1614, the merchants sent out two expeditions that succeeded in mapping much of Hudson Bay. In 1614, Bylot received a commission from the company to take the *Discoverie* out again, this time to see if a passage might be found leading northward out of the bay. His chief pilot, responsible for all navigation and mapping, was William Baffin, an experienced arctic explorer who had sailed for the Muscovy Company before signing on with Bylot. Unfortunately, the voyagers found the waters at the north end of Hudson Bay blocked by ice and shallow water. Baffin kept extremely careful records of his observations, made an accurate map of the region, and also made the first recorded attempt to determine longitude by measuring the moon's displacement from other celestial objects, a theory advanced in Germany in the 15th century. On his return in September 1614, Baffin informed the heads of the Northwest Passage Company that if there were "any passage [west of] Resolution Iland, it is but som creeke or in lett, but the mayne will be upp [Davis Strait]."

The Northwest Passage Company sent Bylot and Baffin out again in the spring of 1616 to test Baffin's idea. Throughout the months of May and June, the trusty *Discoverie* sailed up the western coast of Greenland, past miles of ice-covered cliffs and ranges of snow-covered mountains. When the explorers reached the area of Sanderson's Hope, they headed west, only to be blocked by the same long ice stream that had frustrated Davis. Instead of turning south, however, Bylot and Baffin decided to continue sailing northward. The waters to the north remained sufficiently free of ice for the *Discoverie* to make good progress, and Baffin began to hope that a successful passage could be made. In late June and early July, the shoreline began to curve westward, closing off their path to the north, and Bylot adjusted his course accordingly. Just over 400 miles up the Greenland coast from Sanderson's Hope, the explorers discovered a broad, ice-choked inlet leading north, near the site of the modern Greenland town of Thule. Baffin and Bylot named the opening Sir Thomas Smith's Sound and continued to follow the icy coastline as it curved west, then south. On the west side of Baffin Bay, as the sea north of the Davis Strait is now known, the *Discoverie* passed two more large inlets, first Jones Sound, between Ellesmere and Devon islands, then, on July 12, the entrance to Lancaster Sound, between Devon Island and the great island that now bears Baffin's name. Both inlets appeared too narrow and full of ice to be safe for commercial shipping; Baffin and Bylot were looking for a broad, free passage on the scale of Davis Strait itself. Despite a huge ice shelf that sometimes forced him out of sight of land, Bylot tried to follow the coastline of Baffin Island southward, but when the *Discoverie* reached the region of Cumberland Sound, Bylot and Baffin gave up the search and headed for England.

The failure of the expedition convinced Baffin that no

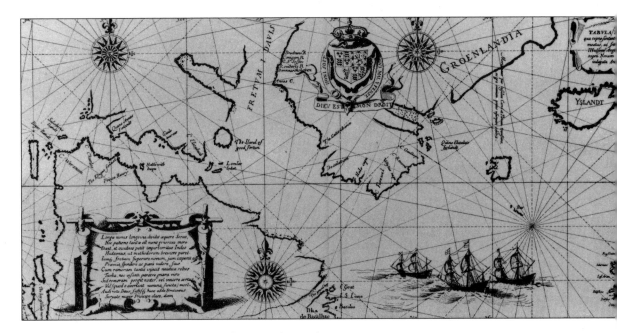

useful northwestern route to China for merchant shipping existed. After the *Discoverie*'s return, he wrote to one of the Northwest Passage Company's members that "there is no passage nor hope of passage in the north of Davis' Straits. We have coasted all, or neere all the circumference thereof and finde it to be no other than a great bay." He advised the company to give up the search in that area and instead pursue the readier profits available to them in the north from whale and walrus hunting. In accordance with his own advice, he abandoned arctic exploration in favor of a career with the British East India Company, but service in the Orient could be as hazardous as the search for the Northwest Passage: Baffin was killed in an assault on the Iranian city of Qeshm, near Hormuz, in 1622. His disillusionment heralded a change in interest on the part of his native land. For most of the next two centuries, England's emphasis would shift from the attempt to discover new trade routes, such as the Northwest Passage, to the colonization and exploitation of known lands, chief among them its fledgling settlements in North America.

The first map showing Hudson's northern discoveries was published in Amsterdam, the Netherlands, in 1612. Because Hudson had once sailed for the Dutch, there was keen interest in his voyage in the Netherlands.

A Tragic Triumph

England's colonial adventure in North America culminated in 1783 with its defeat by the rebellious United States of America, as the republic created from the former 13 colonies joyously styled itself. In the interim, the search for the Northwest Passage took on a new dimension. Baffin's certainty all but discouraged further investigation in the area of the Davis Strait, and England's victory over France in the Seven Years' War gave it, among other prizes, a strong foothold in India, making the discovery of a new route to the East that much less pressing for English merchants. After almost three centuries, the Northwest Passage still held its allure for mariners enamored of adventure, but now more as the object of an intellectual quest than as a sure route to riches and glory. By the middle of the 18th century, many of the great questions about the earth's geography had been answered, and it grew increasingly apparent with each passing year that a passage to Asia above or through the northern extremities of the North American continent would be of little practical import. But the thinkers of the Enlightenment, as the intellectual movement that dominated European thought at this time was known, prized knowledge for its own sake; the Northwest Passage, as one of the last great geographical riddles, therefore continued to exert a considerable pull.

In 1745, England's legislative body, Parliament, voted to award 20,000 pounds to the commander of the first

Sir John Franklin, commander of several of Britain's most important arctic expeditions in the first half of the 19th century, was a decorated veteran of the battles of Trafalgar and New Orleans, but he was not well suited for exploration. In the course of Franklin's 1819 expedition, a Canadian Indian chief named Akaitcho was so moved by the foolhardiness of a course of action proposed by Franklin that he agreed to let some of his Indians accompany the Englishman, in order, as he put it, that "it shall not be said that we permitted you to die alone."

English ship to find a useful passage between the Atlantic and the Pacific. Captain James Cook, the estimable English seaman who had already won fame for his exploration of the Pacific and the Antarctic Circle, was among those who answered the challenge. Cook tried a new strategy—approaching the Arctic regions from the Pacific Ocean. Although his voyage, which lasted from 1776 to 1779, added immeasurably to the store of knowledge available about North America's northwest regions, Cook did not succeed in finding the passage before ice forced him to reverse his course. His journey also proved to be his last, for after putting in for repairs at the island of Hawaii, which he was the first European to discover, Cook was killed by natives. The overland expeditions of other 18th-century explorers—such as Samuel Hearne, an iron-willed 24-year-old Englishman who in 1770–71 traveled from a fur-trader's outpost on the western shore of Hudson Bay to the mouth of the Coppermine River at the Arctic Ocean, and Alexander Mackenzie, a rugged Scotsman who in 1789 traipsed more than 2,000 miles from Lake Athabasca along the course of the Mackenzie River to the Arctic Ocean—while exceptional in many regards, were no more successful than Cook's had been in forcing the Northwest Passage to yield its secrets.

After 1815, England found itself in a unique position. That year marked the final defeat of Napoléon Bonaparte, under whose leadership the armies of France had overrun most of Europe, leaving England isolated. English naval power, in part, enabled it to hold out, but after Napoléon's fall, England no longer had to concern itself to the same degree with France. The end of more than 100 years of unceasing rivalry and frequent warfare between the French and the English left the island nation in a singular situation: Possessed of the world's strongest navy, England now had to find something for it to do.

Among the busywork the overlords of the British Empire devised was a time-honored challenge—the search for the

Northwest Passage. For many, the quest remained, as Martin Frobisher had called it three centuries earlier, "the only thing left undone whereby a notable mind might be made famous and remarkable." Its successful completion, it was hoped, would contribute both scientific knowledge and enhance England's image as a sea power. In the words of John Barrow, second secretary of the Admiralty (the government department responsible for the navy), the search was "in every way worthy of a great and prosperous and enlightened nation; having for its primary object that of the advancement of science, for its own sake." There were also new reasons to believe that this time the search would prove successful. In 1817, William Scoresby, an English whaling captain, reported that more than 18,000 square miles of pack ice off Greenland had disappeared, possibly opening up new arctic routes. Scoresby also noted that his whalers had removed from the blubber of their captured quarry harpoons used exclusively in the Pacific— further indication, to his mind, that a sea passage connected the world's two greatest oceans. (The Arctic was in Scoresby's blood; his father, also a whaling captain, had reached the northernmost latitude ever recorded.)

The Royal Navy's first Northwest Passage expedition left England in April 1818 under Commander John Ross, an even-tempered Scotsman. Ross's voyage duplicated the Bylot and Baffin voyage of 1616 and entered Lancaster Sound, but despite the considerable scientific achievements of his voyage, Ross's failure to locate the passage— he cut his voyage short because he claimed to have seen a chain of rugged hills, which he named the Croker Mountains, that sealed off Lancaster Sound—left him open to considerable ridicule, particularly at the hands of Barrow, for whom the passage had become something of a personal Holy Grail. A follow-up expedition, led by the commander of one of Ross's ships, William Edward Parry, was more successful. Convinced that Ross's reconnaissance of Lancaster Sound was insufficient, Parry took his two ships

Sir John Ross missed out on a prime opportunity to discover the Northwest Passage when he thought he saw a mountain range that closed off Lancaster Sound. No such range exists; Ross had most likely been fooled by the reflections of the sun's rays off icebergs. Although Ross endured much ridicule for his mistake, he distinguished himself on several later arctic expeditions.

George Back, who accompanied Franklin on his first and second overland expeditions, drew this picture of a young Eskimo woman, a member of a tribe living west of the Mackenzie River.

across the sound and through Barrow Strait and into Viscount Melville Sound, both of which he is credited with discovering. In the process Parry explored the coasts of Somerset, Devon, Cornwallis, Bathurst, and Melville islands—the latter four are part of what are known today as the Parry Islands—before pack ice halted his westward progress and forced him and his hardy companions to spend the winter in a harbor off Melville Island. There, in temperatures that hovered consistently near 40 degrees below zero, Parry and his men amused themselves with sing-alongs to the accompaniment of a barrel organ the commander had had the foresight to drag along, by staging theatrical productions of popular comedies of the day, and by publishing a newspaper. They arrived home in England in 1820 to discover themselves heroes, the sharers of a 5,000-pound prize given by Parliament for being the first to cross 110 degrees west latitude. Parry's expedition had revealed more about the American Arctic than any foray since Baffin's; more importantly, it seemed to indicate that to the west of Lancaster Sound and Barrow Strait only ice, and not land, prevented a successful navigation of the Northwest Passage.

In 1819, the same year that Parry departed, the Admiralty sent another of its officers, John Franklin, on an overland expedition to explore the Arctic coast of North America. Simple, cheerful, and humble, the 33-year-old Franklin, a veteran of the Napoleonic Wars, had many friends within the naval hierarchy, which apparently was his chief qualification for this particular assignment. A stranger to hard exercise, Franklin was, moreover, without experience in land travel, but the Admiralty considered an officer of the British navy equal to any imaginable task. Disdaining the warnings of, among others, the experienced fur traders of the Hudson's Bay Company, which maintained outposts across the Far North, the navy sent Franklin into the Arctic with inadequate equipment and preparation. Although Franklin succeeded in carrying out his mission—to retrace Hearne's route from Hudson Bay to the mouth of the Coppermine River and then explore eastward along the coast of Coronation Gulf—during the second winter he and his men were forced to spend in the wild, starvation claimed 11 individuals, and 2 more were murdered. (The killers were unhinged by hunger and starvation.) Most likely all involved would have perished from starvation and cold had it not been for the heroism of midshipman George Back, who trekked hundreds of miles on snowshoes across the frozen tundra in the dead of winter in a successful attempt to obtain help from a friendly band of Copper Indians. The grim predicament of the Englishmen was brought about because of Franklin's persistence in following his orders to the letter—he insisted on taking canoes to the soon-to-be frozen waters of Coronation Gulf despite the imminent onset of winter and the warnings of the Indians and fur traders who at that point were accompanying the expedition. Having almost died himself,

Sir John Ross drew this sketch of his ship, the Victory, *entrapped in ice off the Boothia Peninsula in the winter of 1829. He and his men spent three years stranded aboard the icebound vessel before abandoning ship and making their way, by sled and boat, to Baffin Bay and rescue.*

Franklin referred to the journey as "our long, fatiguing, and disastrous travels in North America"; he dubbed the fort where his party wintered "the House of Misery, Lamentation, and Woe." Nevertheless, he took immense satisfaction in his party's having covered 5,500 miles of the Canadian wilderness.

Both Franklin and the Admiralty remained undaunted by his travails, and in 1825 he was given command of a second overland expedition. Franklin's team spent two years exploring the length of the Mackenzie River and mapping the coast from Alaska to the mouth of the Coppermine. He returned to England a hero and was knighted for his exploits.

Northwest exploration, it was now clear to ambitious and adventurous Englishmen, was a means to build a career. Seeking to rehabilitate his reputation, John Ross set off on a privately financed search for the Northwest Passage in 1829. Ross's hope for success rested on his ship, the *Victory*, which at 150 tons was less than half the size of the vessels recently used in the quest for the strait. Of even greater importance was that the *Victory* had been

This drawing of Eskimo building igloos was based on Ross's account of his 1829–33 expedition. Unlike many British explorers in the Arctic, Ross admired the Eskimo's ingenuity in adapting to their harsh environment and believed that the British could benefit from studying the survival techniques of the native peoples of the north.

equipped with a steam engine, a relatively recent invention, which Ross was convinced would generate enough power to break through the ice that had halted the progress of previous explorers. But Ross soon learned that even had the engine not broken down, forcing him to order it dismantled and abandoned on Boothia Peninsula (Booth was the family name of the gin distiller who had underwritten the voyage), arctic ice was a much more formidable obstacle than anyone who had not experienced it firsthand could imagine. He wrote:

> In a winter's storm the term ice conveys no idea of what it is the fate of an Arctic navigator to witness and to feel. But let them remember that ice is stone. Then let them imagine, if they can, these mountains of crystal hurled through a narrow strait by a rapid tide; meeting, as mountains in motion would meet, with the noise of thunder, breaking from each other's precipices huge fragments, or rending each other asunder till, losing their former equilibrium, they fall over headlong, lifting the sea around in breakers, and whirling it in eddies.

By the end of September 1829, this frigid barrier had halted the *Victory's* southward progress along the Boothia Peninsula. The ship remained trapped in ice in the Gulf of Boothia for the next three years; in all that period, it was able to move less than five miles. All but one of Ross's crew of 23 men were able to survive the ordeal by emulating the practices of the Eskimo, with whom they enjoyed particularly amicable relations. Ross had his men replicate the Eskimo way of dressing, and they subsisted on a similar diet of fish and seal meat, high in fresh oil and fats, which the Eskimo relied on in the absence of fresh vegetables. Although Ross was fascinated by the Eskimo, he also insisted that his men maintain as many of the customs of home as possible, believing that to do so would strengthen morale and overcome boredom. Prayer services were held on Sunday, and Ross ordered each of the men to take a daily constitutional along a sand path he had made on top of the packed ice and snow on deck. Despite such measures, boredom and despair were inevitable. "Today was as yesterday, and as was today, so would be tomorrow," Ross wrote, and his men "grew weary for want of occupation, for want of variety, for want of thought." There were occasions for joy—hunting trips made by sled, sometimes in the company of the Eskimo; the successful overland sled expedition carried out by Ross's nephew and second-in-command, James Clark Ross, to discover the location of the north magnetic pole—but even as he struggled to remain optimistic, Ross could not avoid reaching some grim conclusions. "Amid all its brilliancy," he wrote, "this land, the land of ice and snow, has ever been and ever will be a dull dreary, heart-sinking, monotonous waste, under the influence of which the very mind is paralyzed, ceasing to care or think."

Even so, Ross kept his wits about him, and when provisions began to run low during the winter of 1831–32, the third he and his men had spent in the icy fastness, Ross made plans to abandon the *Victory* come spring. On foot and on sled, Ross and his men, some of them sick, others weak from hunger, some snow blind, made their way across the ice to a beach on Somerset Island, where four years earlier, as the captain knew, Parry had jettisoned several hundred pounds of burdensome supplies. There, in Somerset House, an improvised 31-by-16-foot structure of wood and canvas insulated with ice walls 4 feet thick, they spent the long winter of 1832–33. In the summer, they were able to take to the water of Prince Regent Inlet in boats dragged from the *Victory*. Making their way carefully through the breaking ice of Barrow Strait and Lancaster Sound, they reached Baffin Bay in mid-August, where they flagged down a whaling ship, the *Isabella*— one of the two vessels commanded by Ross on his discredited voyage 15 years earlier. Its crew initially refused to believe Ross when he identified himself—Ross and all his men, the sailors of the *Isabella* informed the emaciated, disheveled collection of castaways, had perished two years

earlier. Resurrected, Ross and his men were returned to England, where they were celebrated by the public, by Parliament, and by the king himself.

Perhaps because Ross had so clearly demonstrated the considerable risks involved in the search for the Northwest Passage without producing any tangible benefits—for all his undeniable heroism, Ross had provided little new information—it was some time before the Admiralty again mounted a new probe in the Arctic. When the Admiralty did unveil plans for its new expedition in 1844—the indefatigable armchair admiral John Barrow declaring that "after having opened the East and West doors, [England] would be laughed at by all the world for having hesitated to cross the threshold"—it had several veterans of the search from which to choose in appointing a commander. Among them was Franklin, who after a disillusioning six-year stint as governor of the British penal colony on Tasmania was desperate to return to the frigid wilderness.

While trapped aboard the Victory, Ross's men and the local Eskimo developed a close friendship. The Eskimo regularly came to the ship to trade and visit, and the English made regular social calls at the Eskimo village. Sporting contests were conducted on the ice, and both groups vied to demonstrate the superiority of their methods of hunting and fishing. This watercolor, from a drawing by Ross, shows two Eskimos, Ikmalick and Apelagliu, drawing a map of the water routes west in the Victory's *stateroom.*

There were factors weighing against his selection, such as his advancing age (59), his expanding girth, and his general lack of physical conditioning, not to mention the considerable qualifications of other candidates, such as Parry and the Rosses. Franklin prevailed, however, for John Ross was even older than he was and was still disliked by Barrow; James Clark Ross had promised his new bride that he would explore no more; and Parry, who was officially retired, told Barrow that "if you don't let him go the man will die of disappointment."

Franklin's orders were to search for a link between the northern channel discovered by Parry and the coastal waterways he had explored; failing that, he was to look north for a passage. To do so, he was given two large warships, fitted with both sails and two 20-horsepower steam engines: the 340-ton *Erebus* and the 370-ton *Terror*, both veteran polar campaigners. The two vessels carried the best the navy could supply: fine china and cut glass, enormous libraries, dress uniforms, and mahogany furniture. They carried as well equipment more useful for northern exploration, although, despite Ross's example, Franklin made no provision for hunting fresh game. Everybody concerned felt that such a well-equipped expedition, manned by England's finest, could not fail.

On May 19, 1845, the two warships, gleaming in fresh black paint with a jaunty yellow stripe along their gunports, left the mouth of the Thames. Franklin's wife, Lady Jane, watched from shore as her husband waved a handkerchief from the *Erebus*. The last sighting of the expedition came in June, when whalers sighted the two ships at the entrance to Lancaster Sound. Two winters passed with no further word. In late 1847, John Ross, who had promised Franklin to personally lead a search party if one became necessary, suggested a rescue expedition, pointing out that if Franklin were still in the Arctic his supplies would be running low, but officials of the Admiralty refused to heed Ross's warning. When the spring of 1848 came and went with no word, however, their attitude changed. The government offered 20,000 pounds for Franklin's rescue and half that amount for anyone with news of the expedition's fate.

The navy dispatched three relief expeditions in 1848, one to follow Franklin through Lancaster Sound, one to search the Pacific entrance, and one overland party. Several factors hindered the effectiveness of the rescue mission. The searchers possessed an incomplete understanding of the arctic climate and failed to realize, for example, that a channel frozen solid one year might be free the next. Admiralty politics and cronyism meant that information from outsiders, such as whalers, hunters, and Eskimo, was ignored. Nonetheless, it was determined that Franklin had not penetrated west of the Mackenzie River. In the brutally cold winter of 1848–49, James Clark Ross, in command of the Atlantic search party, found Peel Sound, the channel between Somerset and Prince of Wales islands, to be totally blocked by ice. Despite his

The desperate men of the Victory *row toward rescue aboard the whaler* Isabella, *which Ross had once commanded, in the summer of 1833.*

The Erebus *and the* Terror, *both under the general command of Sir John Franklin, set sail for the Northwest Passage in May 1845. Both vessels had formerly been used by the Royal Navy as bomb ships, meaning that they carried shell-firing mortars. The* Terror *had visited the Arctic once before, under the command of George Back.*

considerable arctic experience—he had commanded several voyages of his own after his adventure with his uncle—Ross never considered that the channel might have been open for Franklin, nor did he have any way of knowing that 1846, when Franklin had reached the sound, had been freakishly warm. He declared that Franklin could not have sailed south from Barrow Strait. This convinced naval officials that the lost explorer must have followed his secondary orders to seek a northern passage.

Lady Jane remained convinced that her husband lived. Franklin's shy, soft-spoken, but beautiful and intelligent spouse now revealed uncommon courage and persistence. She interviewed whaling captains for news and wrote streams of letters to world leaders, including President Zachary Taylor of the United States, pleading for aid and rescue expeditions. Her efforts made her a national heroine, and public sympathy placed enormous pressure on the Admiralty to save British honor by rescuing the lost explorers.

In 1850, 12 ships, including 2 sent by Americans in response to Lady Jane's pleas, headed for the North American Arctic. All planned to concentrate on the waters north and west of Barrow Strait. Dozens of English sailors, harnessed to heavy sledges, spread out across the frozen wastes. Flares were fired, marker balloons were released, huge messages were painted on rocky cliffs, caches of supplies were left, and letters were even tied to the tails of foxes in the hope that Franklin's men would discover them. In August, searchers located the remains of a Royal Navy encampment on Beechey Island, off the southwestern coast of Devon Island. Tent foundations, empty food tins, and the graves of three seamen revealed the camp to have been Franklin's winter quarters. The rescue teams found no clues, however, to the lost ships' fate.

One of the expeditions sent out in 1850 consisted of two ships under Richard Collinson detailed to explore the Pacific entrance. Collinson's junior commander was an ambitious, moody 26-year-old officer named Robert McClure who had served as a lieutenant on James Clark Ross's rescue mission. Hoping to single-handedly rescue Franklin and to be the first through the Northwest Passage, McClure, without authorization, sailed his ship, the 400-ton *Investigator*, on an uncharted course through the Aleutian Islands, around the northwest coast of Alaska and on eastward. While the wall of the permanent polar pack gleamed only 90 miles to the north, the impatient McClure used the *Investigator* as a battering ram to force a passage through the ice, working his way slowly past the Mackenzie River delta, where he met puzzled Eskimo who had never before seen a white man. As a mass of moving ice carried the *Investigator* northeast up the narrow strait between Banks and Victoria islands, McClure recorded in his journal his hopes for a successful link with Viscount Melville Sound, where Parry's quest had ended. All references to finding Franklin disappeared, but on September 17 new ice halted the *Investigator*'s progress some 60 miles from Melville Sound.

By the beginning of October, ice had frozen McClure in place. After sealing and covering his ship in preparation for winter, he set out on a sledge journey with a few of his men along the eastern shore of Banks Island. On October 26, he reached Viscount Melville Sound, confirming for the first time the existence of a water passage between the Atlantic and the Pacific oceans. The following summer McClure tried again to make the passage, only to be blocked by the same polar ice stream that had frustrated Parry in 1820. An attempt to round Banks Island through the strait that now bears McClure's name ended with the *Investigator* frozen in a small bay on the coast of the island, just short of its goal.

There the ship remained trapped in unbroken whiteness for two winters, a living hell for its crew, who fell victim to scurvy, hunger, boredom, and the tensions of isolation. By the winter of 1852–53, four had gone insane and had to be restrained in irons. In March 1853, McClure reluctantly prepared to abandon the vessel and head overland for rescue. On April 6, however, a party from an expedition to the east discovered the gaunt, starving men. The meeting of the rescuers and the haggard men of the *Investigator* marked the somewhat anticlimactic—if not for McClure and his crew—completion of the search for the Northwest Passage, as it marked the first time that an expedition from the east had hooked up with an expedition from the west. McClure's party abandoned the *Investigator*; he and his men were brought by sledge across the ice to where British ships waited off the southern coast of Melville Island.

McClure and his crew received a prize of 10,000 pounds from Parliament for their discovery of the passage. With the great Arctic mystery apparently solved, public and official interest in Franklin's fate waned. In 1854, the navy officially declared him and his crew dead, but Lady Jane continued the battle to discover her husband's end and kept ceaseless pressure on the Admiralty to renew the search. Knowing her husband as she did, she continued to believe that Franklin, despite the official line, had followed his original orders, had sailed south from Barrow Strait, and would therefore be found somewhere near the southern end of Peel Sound.

In April 1854, John Rae, a surgeon for the Hudson's Bay Company, met a group of Eskimo while on a trip up the eastern coast of Boothia Peninsula. Rae, an inveterate hiker of the arctic wilderness, had participated in the Franklin search, but he was scorned by the navy because of his espousal of native survival methods. The Eskimo told him a story about a group of 35 to 40 white men who had starved to death near the mouth of the Great Fish River, south of King William Island, and they showed him silverware, coins, and other relics that could only have come from Franklin's ships. Rae quickly sent word to England. In 1856 another Hudson's Bay Company explorer found more relics, including a backgammon board that Lady Jane herself remembered putting aboard the *Erebus*. When the Admiralty refused her demands for an expedition to investigate these leads, Lady Jane used her dwindling funds to purchase a small steam yacht and asked Leopold McClintock, who like McClure had served as an officer under James Clark Ross, to find the truth about her husband's fate. McClintock, who along with his officers refused to accept any payment for his services, was commissioned not only to discover what had happened to Franklin but to seek evidence that he had reached the region near the mouth of the Back River, which would mean that he had been the first to discover the link that

Lady Jane Franklin at age 22; the illustration is a facsimile of the only portrait of her known to exist. Lady Jane knew her husband well; she alone maintained, correctly, that Franklin would have obeyed his orders and sailed south from the Barrow Strait.

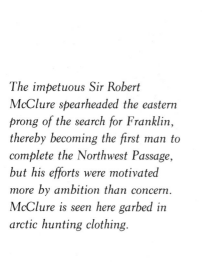

The impetuous Sir Robert McClure spearheaded the eastern prong of the search for Franklin, thereby becoming the first man to complete the Northwest Passage, but his efforts were motivated more by ambition than concern. McClure is seen here garbed in arctic hunting clothing.

completed the Northwest Passage. (Named after George Back, who had himself led several rescue voyages, the Back River connected, via the Great Slave Lake, with the Mackenzie River, which, as Franklin's second expedition had demonstrated, provided an outlet to the Arctic Ocean and points west.)

Reliable and even temperered, beloved by his men, the 38-year-old McClintock was ideally suited for his task. In 1857, 12 years after Franklin first set sail, he set off to discover what had happened. While spending the winter of 1858–59 on Somerset Island, he encountered Eskimo with relics and tales of starving white men "who fell down and died as they walked along," skeletons, and ships crushed by ice. Finding Peel Sound again blocked by ice, McClintock sent out a series of sledge expeditions to explore the coasts of Boothia Peninsula, Prince of Wales Island, and King William Island. As he traveled southward, McClintock heard stories of emaciated men hauling boats overland and dying as they walked. On May 24, 1859, on King William Island, McClintock's sledge party discovered the skeleton of a young officer's servant lying facedown on a windswept ridge. Later that day, he found a message from another of his search parties saying that a letter from the lost expedition had been found at Victory Point, on the island's northwestern coast.

McClintock hurried north. He soon stumbled on the remains of a wood-and-iron sledge that carried a heavy ship's boat. The boat contained books, towels, soap, silver plate, shoes, watches, and cigars. On top of all lay the skeletons of two sailors. When he reached Victory Point, the appalled McClintock saw further evidence that Franklin's dying men had lost the ability to think clearly. Sledges lay scattered about, loaded with 10 tons of gear, including button polish and curtain rods. The sailors had obviously intended to haul this useless material themselves and had abandoned the loads when it became clear that they could not manage what would be suicidal even for healthy men.

The letter found at Victory Point consisted of two messages scrawled on a standard Admiralty report form. The first, dated May 28, 1847, stated that Franklin, finding Peel Sound at first blocked, had sailed north up Wellington Channel and around Cornwallis Island before spending the winter of 1845–46 on Beechey Island. The next summer he had managed to penetrate Peel Sound as far as the northern tip of King William Island before being trapped in ice. All hands expected that with the coming of summer they would be able to complete the passage. The second message presented a grimmer picture. Written on April 27, 1848, it revealed that Franklin had died in June

1847, that the ships had been trapped in ice for 19 months, and that 24 men had died. Franklin's second-in-command, Captain F. R. M. Crozier, had decided to abandon the ships and march overland for the mouth of the Great Fish River in hopes of meeting a rescue expedition.

The exact cause of Franklin's death was never found. Scurvy clearly brought about the death of most of his crew. The navy had learned neither from James Cook's discoveries of the previous century regarding preventive measures against the disease (a diet of fresh food high in vitamin C) nor from the practices of the Eskimo. Calmly certain that British civilization was superior in all environments and that the Royal Navy could master any challenge, the Admiralty sent large, oceangoing warships, loaded with all the trappings of Victorian society, into the shallow, ice-filled channels of the Arctic. The 20th-century explorer

Sir Leopold McClintock donated his services to Lady Jane Franklin to help with the search for her missing husband. It was McClintock's expedition that discovered the evidence of the tragic end of the Franklin voyage.

Vilhjalmur Stefansson believed that Franklin's party "died because they brought their environment with them; they were not prepared . . . to adapt to another." Franklin himself never reached the last link in his passage, but as they struggled, dying, along the coast of King William Island and across the ice onto the frozen mainland, many of his men did. Although she had long since begun to live with the knowledge that her husband would never return, Lady Jane at least had the satisfaction of witnessing him undergo a kind of resurrection—posthumous acclaim as the discoverer of the Northwest Passage. Even in death, Franklin was of service to his country, for the 11-year search for him added immensely to the store of knowledge about the North American Arctic, particularly the Arctic islands.

Franklin's tragic triumph is in many ways a fitting climax to the story of the search for the Northwest Passage, attributable as it was to all that was best and worst in his character. The Englishman's bulldog tenacity enabled him to achieve all that he did, but at the same time his certainty in the rightness of his actions caused him to make fatal errors—mistakes that he and the unfortunate members of his crew would not be given the opportunity to learn from. But Franklin was not the first to be tragically beguiled by the icy siren song of the Northwest Passage. For four centuries, the quest had held the imagination by appealing to humankind's greatness—its courage, vision, endurance, ingenuity, curiosity—and to its folly—its vanity, greed, egotism, and vaingloriousness. Franklin's triumph belonged not to him alone but to McClure and Rae, McClintock, Parry, the Rosses, Baffin and Bylot, Hudson, Frobisher, Cartier, Verrazano, Cabot, and all the unnamed other explorers for whom the piles of discarded clothing and supplies, the timbers of wrecked ships and boats, and the frozen bones of skeletons scattered about the frigid north serve as a grim memorial to their weakness and strength.

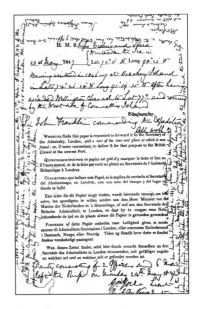

This document was found in a cairn on the western coast of King William Island in the spring of 1859 by McClintock's expedition. The printed material is a standard Admiralty form, composed in six languages, requesting the finder to return it to the nearest British government official. The handwritten material constitutes two separate messages, dated May 24, 1847, and April 25, 1848. The latter reports the abandonment of Franklin's 2 ships, his death and the death of 24 members of his party, and the determination of the remainder of the expedition to head for the Great Fish River.

Further Reading

Berton, Pierre. *The Arctic Grail: The Quest for the Northwest Passage.* New York: Viking Penguin, 1988.

Bettex, Albert. *The Discovery of the World.* New York: Simon & Schuster, 1960.

Bourne, Edward G. *The Northmen, Columbus, and Cabot.* New York: Scribners, 1906.

Burrage, Henry S., ed. *Early English and French Voyages, Chiefly from Hakluyt, 1534–1608.* New York: Barnes & Noble, 1967.

Cumming, W. P., R. A. Shelton, and D. B. Quinn. *The Discovery of North America.* New York: American Heritage Press, 1972.

Day, Alan E. *Search for the Northwest Passage.* New York: Garland, 1986.

Durant, Will. *The Age of Faith.* New York: Simon & Schuster, 1950.

———. *The Reformation.* New York: Simon & Schuster, 1950.

Hakluyt, Richard. *Voyages.* Reprint of 1600 edition. New York: Viking Press, 1965.

Kippes, A. *A Narrative of the Voyages Round the World Performed by Captain James Cook.* Philadelphia: Coates, n.d.

Lehane, Brendan. *The Northwest Passage.* Alexandria, VA: Time-Life Books, 1981.

Maclean, Alistair. *Captain Cook.* Garden City, NY: Doubleday, 1972.

Morison, Samuel Eliot. *The European Discovery of America.* Vols. 1 and 2. New York: Oxford University Press, 1971.

Norman, Charles. *The Discovery of North America.* New York: Crowell, 1834.

Stefansson, Vilhjalmur, ed. *Great Adventurers and Explorations*. New York: Dial Press, 1947.

Villiers, Alan. *Captain James Cook*. New York: Scribners, 1967.

Wright, Louis B., and Elaine W. Fowler, eds. *West and by North*. New York: Delacorte, 1971.

Wroth, Lawrence C. *The Voyages of Giovanni da Verrazzano*. New Haven: Yale University Press, 1970.

Chronology

Entries in roman type refer directly to the exploration of the Northwest Passage; entries in italics refer to important historical and cultural events of the era.

1095–1291	*Pope Urban II urges Christians to fight the Muslim infidel, thereby launching the Crusades; European contact with Near Eastern and Middle Eastern peoples spawns dependency on eastern trade routes*
1298	*Marco Polo writes of his travels to the Orient, thus creating a great demand for Eastern commodities*
1453	*Constantinople, the last bulwark holding open routes of Christian trade with the East, falls to the Turks; a new trade route to the East is sought*
1492	*Christopher Columbus discovers the New World in an attempt to reach the Indies by sailing west*
1494	*Treaty of Tordesillas divides western discoveries into Portuguese and Spanish spheres of influence*
1497	John Cabot, a Genoan, sails under the English flag and discovers Newfoundland
1498	*Portuguese explorer Vasco da Gama rounds the Cape of Good Hope, at the southern tip of Africa, and creates a new trade route to the Indies*
1519–22	*Ferdinand Magellan becomes the first man to circumnavigate the globe*
1524	Giovanni da Verrazano, sailing for the French, explores the North American coast from the Carolinas to Newfoundland looking for a passage west
1534–36	Jacques Cartier extends the French search for a passage into the Gulf of St. Lawrence and the St. Lawrence River
1576–78	Martin Frobisher explores Frobisher Bay and Baffin Island for Queen Elizabeth I of England; enters Hudson Bay by mistake

1585–87   John Davis maps Davis Strait and guesses correctly the exact location of the entrance to the Northwest Passage

1609–11   Henry Hudson explores Atlantic seaboard of North America for the Dutch and English and discovers the river and bay that bear his name; set adrift in Hudson Bay by mutineers

1776–79   Captain James Cook tries and fails to penetrate a Pacific entrance to the passage

1819–23   Lt. William Parry explores Lancaster Sound and sails through the passage as far as Melville Island

1845   Departure of ill-fated Franklin expedition from Dartmouth, England; officers and crew trapped off King William Island by ice; all are dead by 1848

1850–54   While searching for Franklin, Robert McClure penetrates the Pacific entrance as far as Banks Island; completes Northwest Passage partially by sled

1859   Leopold McClintock discovers the remains of the Franklin expedition

Index

Picture Credits

Warren Brown currently resides in Astoria, New York. He has a B.A. from the New England Conservatory of Music and a physics degree from Tufts University.

William H. Goetzmann holds the Jack S. Blanton, Sr., Chair in History at the University of Texas at Austin, where he has taught for many years. The author of numerous works on American history and exploration, he won the 1967 Pulitzer and Parkman prizes for his *Exploration and Empire: The Role of the Explorer and Scientist in the Winning of the American West, 1800–1900*. With his son William N. Goetzmann, he coauthored *The West of the Imagination*, which received the Carr P. Collins Award in 1986 from the Texas Institute of Letters. His documentary television series of the same name received a blue ribbon in the history category at the American Film and Video Festival held in New York City in 1987. A recent work, *New Lands, New Men: America and the Second Great Age of Discovery*, was published in 1986 to much critical acclaim.

Michael Collins served as command module pilot on the *Apollo 11* space mission, which landed his colleagues Neil Armstrong and Buzz Aldrin on the moon. A graduate of the United States Military Academy, Collins was named an astronaut in 1963. In 1966 he piloted the *Gemini 10* mission, during which he became the third American to walk in space. The author of several books on space exploration, Collins was director of the Smithsonian Institution's National Air and Space Museum from 1971 to 1978 and is a recipient of the Presidential Medal of Freedom.